WORSHIP MENTORS

THE STRATEGIES, LESSONS, AND ADVICE OF THE WORLD'S MOST INFLUENTIAL WORSHIP LEADERS.

SHALON PALMER

Founder, Worship Online

Worship Mentors

Worship Mentors

The Strategies, Lessons, and Advice of the World's Most Influential Worship Leaders

Copyright © 2021 by Worship Online Inc.

All rights reserved.

No part of this publication may be reproduced, stored in a retrieval system, stored in a database and/or published in any form or by any means, electronic, mechanical, photocopying, recording or otherwise, without the prior written permission of the publisher.

www.worshiponline.com

Thank you to all of our mentors for graciously sharing your time and wisdom to help resource the global church. This wouldn't have been possible without you.

Contents

—

Introduction 10

How to Read This Book 15

    Tasha Cobbs Leonard 28

    Alexander Pappas 34

    Jake France 38

    Phil Joel 44

    Jon Egan 50

    Phil Thompson 56

    Josh Miller 60

    Jared Runion & Emily Wyant 64

    Rita Springer 68

Krissy Nordhoff 72

William McDowell 76

Meredith Andrews 82

Katelyn Hill 86

Kim Walker-Smith 92

We The Kingdom 98

Emmy Rose 102

Gable Price 110

Dante Bowe 114

Hillsong UNITED Benjamin Hastings & Dylan Thomas .. 118

Aaron Moses 124

Pat Barrett 128

Matt Redman 134

Kari Jobe 138

Naomi Raine 144

Chris Tomlin 148

Aodhan King 152

Brian Johnson 156

David Leonard 162

Mack Brock 166

Cody Carnes 172

Sarah Reeves 176

Phil Wickham 182

Josh Baldwin 188

Joth Hunt & Sam Evans 192

Jon Foreman 198

Jeremy Camp 204

Amanda Lindsey Cook 208

Sean Curran 212

Andrew Holt 218

Aaron Ivey 222

Danny Gokey 228

Judah Akers 232

Mia Fieldes 236

Kristian Stanfill 242

Conclusion 247

Introduction

Shalon Palmer (Founder/CEO, Worship Online)

—

When I was a rowdy thirteen-year-old growing up in Louisiana, my mom dragged my three brothers and me to church every week. To me, church was this boring place where I was forced to sit through an hour of torture so that we could go eat at Posados Cafe afterward. On Wednesday nights, we had youth group, which was only slightly better because I got to hang out with girls and eat pizza.

One summer, my mom shipped us off to church camp. Not just any church camp, though. This one was called Centrifuge. I was excited because most of my friends were going, and with a name like Centrifuge and a logo that looked like swirling fire, what thirteen-year-old boy wouldn't be excited? What's a couple of hours of boring preaching if that means I get to hang out with my friends and play games all day? Also, I heard there would be girls and pizza.

As someone who had been going to church my entire life, I was generally immune to the tactics of a typical youth worship service. I could go through the most incredible-sounding worship, the hippest-looking youth pastor, or heart-grabbing altar calls. Yet, all I could think about was what I was going to eat after or who would see me lift my hands during worship.

Once camp started, I went through the first couple of days pretty much how you would expect: playing kickball, staring at girls I was too scared to talk to, and eating a lot of pizza. We really took those days for granted, didn't we? Play games, eat, small group, play games, eat, worship service, sleep, and repeat. That pretty much sums it up. However, on the third night, something different happened.

It started off a lot like the hundreds of services I had previously been in. Worship, check; preacher, check; band comes back up at the end, che— wait a second… something was off. There was a tear in my eye. Now, I was a tough kid; I didn't cry for just anyone. So then, why was there a tear in my eye? As I was scrambling to figure out what kind of voodoo I'd been sucked into, I felt a nudge from deep within me say, "I'm real, and I'm here." I couldn't believe it! God?

On the one hand, I was so excited because I was finally experiencing what I'd heard so many people talk about for years. But on the other hand, I was crying in front of my friends. So, I did what any 13-year-old boy would do; I sucked in every bit of emotion I had while screaming on the inside, "Get it together, Shalon! Before someone sees you!" And like the stillness at the top of the roller coaster, before it drops you at 120mph and sends you for a loop, I heard the voice say again, "I'm here, and I'm real. Let go and let me carry you."

In a flash, things I had been holding onto for years began to pour out of me and onto him. Heartbreak, fear, fatherlessness, family abuse, stuff I didn't even know was affecting me started pouring out. At the same time, I felt my heart begin to open. I can only describe the feeling as a thousand-pound weight being lifted off my shoulders as I realized I didn't have to fight against those feelings anymore. This was the first time I had ever experienced or heard from God. I gave my life to Jesus that night and set the foundation for a real relationship with him. After giving my life and burdens to Jesus, I experienced genuine gratitude and worship as we sang for hours into the night.

Now, you may be wondering, "Why did this guy just tell me his personal testimony, which had nothing to do with worship leaders, at the beginning of a book for worship leaders?" And I say, what do you mean? Don't you remember all the parts about the band, the music, and how extraordinary the worship leaders were? No?

EXACTLY!

If you're wondering why the worship leaders weren't a part of the main storyline in my story, Amanda Cook (Pg. 208) has a great explanation:

> "The music in a worship gathering of people is a soundtrack that serves the purpose of the story being unfolded. We can

all walk away with our own stories, and not, 'that song was amazing.' We want to have these epiphanies and experiences with God and then go back to the soundtrack because it supports and reminds us of what we experienced. The song, or the band, wasn't the experience. It just had a supporting role. Worship leaders serve and create a soundtrack to someone else's expression, revelation, window into clarity, and communion with Christ. While not getting in the way or trying to become the main storyline."

When I got home from camp, I asked my mom if I could download every song I could remember from that week. I listened to them on repeat for months. Not because the songs were so awesome or the band played them so spectacularly, but because they were the soundtrack to my personal story of redemption. They reminded me of what God had done in my life. Still to this day, songs like "God of Wonders" and "Indescribable" take me right back to that sweaty auditorium, and I'm reminded of how God wants to carry my burdens. My soundtrack is filled with songs that remind me of different parts of God's heart throughout the years. That's the power of music. It can't be emphasized enough that to be part of an individual's soundtrack that points them to God is a high calling.

While I was having my roller-coaster journey of an experience with God that night, the band played and sang the entire time. Because of their willingness to simply create a soundtrack to my story with God, I'm where I am today, sitting in my office, typing this with tear-stained keys and a grateful heart. I don't remember their names, what they were wearing, or what they looked like. But I remember what God did that night. This, my friends, is the job of a worship leader.

How to Read This Book

—

Abraham Lincoln said, "Give me six hours to chop down a tree, and I'll spend the first four sharpening the ax." In other words, with a bit of preparation, we can accomplish our goals significantly faster and with less stress than if we just went straight to work with a "dull ax." Even the greatest lumberjack would have difficulty chopping down a large tree with a dull ax in six hours.

There's no question that we all understand the importance of stewarding our gifts and talents for the Lord through practice and preparation. The mere fact that you're reading this book right now shows that you're someone who values the gifts inside of you. However, I want us to consider the not-so-obvious question here. As worship leaders, what is our version of "sharpening the ax?"

There are a lot of things Abe could have done to prepare himself to chop down the tree faster. And not all of them are created equal. He could have practiced his swing, measured and analyzed the tree, put a comfortable grip on the ax, and so on. None of those options are wrong. They all would help him chop down the tree. However, there was one option that would allow him to reach his goal faster than the rest. And that was to sharpen his ax.

A mentor of mine used to tell me, "It's not the hours you put into work, but the work you put into the hours." What can we do that will get us the most significant results with the least amount of effort? What's the most effective way to become a better leader, singer, recruiter, musician, organizer, or songwriter? Out of all the ways to sharpen our ax of worship leadership, which of them is the most effective? About six years ago, I came across an answer that changed my life.

When I got my dream job of becoming a worship leader, I was ecstatic. I finally got to do what I loved every day. However, as anyone who gets a job doing something they love knows, it's very easy for that original charm to slowly wear off. After only a few months, I was constantly stressed with the day-to-day of leading, scheduling, preparing, organizing, and rehearsing. Every day was a new conflict with a team member or another staff member. I did everything I knew to make things better and more efficient, but I wasn't having any luck. I felt like I was just spinning my wheels, and nothing was going to change.

One morning on the way to work, I was listening to a personal development and leadership coach named Jim Rohn. A friend suggested him to me, and at this point, I was willing to try anything. Something Jim said struck a nerve in me so much that it caused me to pull over on the side of the road and start intensely jotting notes into my phone. He said, "You're the average of the five people you spend the most time with." I thought, *Hmm, that's interesting.* He continued, "If you hang out with five losers, you'll be the sixth. If you hang out with five winners, you'll be the sixth. If you hang out with five broke people, you'll be the sixth. And if you hang out with five rich people, you'll be the sixth." While Jim was quite blunt in describing this concept, his words were exactly what my hard head needed to hear.

As I started to review my own life to see how accurate his statements were, a lightbulb went off in my head. I didn't really have much ambition in life to do something impactful. And guess what, neither did the people I was spending the most time with. I was also pretty stressed and struggling financially at the time. You can probably guess it, so were the people I was spending the most time with. I had been struggling in my relationships since I could remember. It just so happens that most of my family and closest friends have challenging relationships with their spouses or significant others.

Rohn was exactly right. As I went line by line, the good and the bad, of my life, I could see a clear pattern. Whether you believe this concept to be 100% true or not, there's no denying the influence that the people around you have on your life. The people you spend the most time with shape who you are and determine the types of conversations that dominate your attention. They decide what kinds of attitudes and behaviors you're exposed to. Eventually, you start to think as they think and behave the way they behave. To put it plainly, If you want a positive life, you can't spend all your time with negative people. According to research by Dr. David McClelland of Harvard, the people you habitually associate with determine as much as 95% of your success or failure in life. I don't know about you, but that's a lot.

As I was pulled over on the side of the road in my black Dodge RAM truck, I started to write down the things that I wanted in my life. I wanted a closer relationship with God, to be a better leader, to have deeper relationships with people, to be a better musician, to be more disciplined, to have a healthier body. This list went on. Believing I had all the answers to my problems, I started to get excited. However, that excitement subsided when I realized one critical missing piece of the puzzle. I don't personally know that many people whom I want to be like in those areas. And the few I do know, I can't spend all of my time with them, or they'd get sick of me.

Finally, Jim said this, "The dream in your heart may be bigger than your personal environment." I knew that to be true for me. I had two options: Continue down the path I was going that would eventually lead to me despising my job as a worship leader and maybe even the church itself. Or find a way to surround myself with people that have not only figured out how to do what I want to do effectively but know how to do it with passion, excitement, and excellence every single day. I knew I needed mentors.

Here was where I had my next "ah-ha!" moment. Even though I didn't personally know this man I was listening to over the speakers of my truck, the things he was saying were impacting me right at that moment. I was learning from him, digesting his words, and effectively spending my time with him. He was a mentor.

So, I thought to myself, *I may not personally know enough great leaders to spend most of my time with, but I do know "of" a ton of great leaders.* I went straight to the internet and started googling the leaders I wanted to be like. Quickly, I found books, courses, podcasts, and articles full of all the strategies and wisdom I could possibly need. Over the next few months, I started going through book after book, article after article. In that process, I wasn't just gaining knowledge; I was spending time with these leaders, learning to think as they think, behaving like they behave, and sharpening my ax.

Most importantly, I started spending time with the most outstanding leader of all time—Jesus Christ. If 95% of my life is determined by whom I'm spending my time with, you better believe I'm spending that with Jesus. So much so that I would imagine him sitting in front of me, me asking him questions, and him speaking directly to me as I read his words.

Tasha Cobbs (Pg. 28) said it best when she said:

> "Mentorship is very crucial in my life. A lot of times, people think mentors have to be touched or that they have to be somebody you can reach every single day, but I don't think that's the case. The Bible says for us to study to show ourselves approved, which can be scripture, books, videos, etc. I study people. CeCe Winans was a mentor of mine for many years before I ever met her. I was studying her life because I loved that she walked in integrity. I loved how she loved her husband and her children. So I would encourage everyone to find a mentor. Even if it's someone you can't touch, text, or call. Find someone whose life you can study."

I wanted to be great at leading my team and pointing people to the Lord through music and worship. Once I started surrounding myself with people that were already excellently doing that, my life changed dramatically. I was able to attract, lead, and grow a community of people who desired the heart of God and loved every second of it. I also rediscovered my love for worship, music, and being part of a church. I now have hundreds of mentors in every area of my life, and I'm always finding new people that I can learn from. In no way am I now perfect at anything. I constantly mess up. But you know what? I have mentors for that as well. Every day is a journey of stewarding my gifts and learning more about the heart of God.

This is why we spent the last three years seeking out people we believed would have something to teach us in these areas. Anytime I want to become better at something or break through a glass ceiling holding me back, the first thing I do is find the people that are already the best in the world at what I want to do. Then I surround myself with their advice and wisdom. You may have heard the saying, "If you're the smartest person in the room, you're in the wrong room." Here's a key point to remember: If you want to be average at something, surround yourself with people who are average at it. If you want to be good at something, surround yourself with people that are good at it. However, if your desire is to be great at something, surround yourself with great people. This applies to every single area of your life.

That is why I put this book together. As you read through these pages, you will be surrounded by the words and wisdom of people who have figured out how to have a massive impact on the kingdom. Whether that's through being a worship leader, writing songs, leading their teams, growing a church worship ministry, or many other things. Consider them your mentors.

Before you say, "Well, that person is just a songwriter or artist. He/she doesn't know the first thing about what I have to do every day at my church." Let's not be so quick to discount the advice of someone who has been a part of thousands, even millions, of people's journeys with the Lord. This book isn't to teach you how to be a worship leader or a songwriter, although there's plenty of advice for that in here. It's to allow you to see behind the curtain and get inside the minds of others who have led thousands of people to the Lord through music and songs. This is the way I have found to most effectively sharpen my ax in the area of worship leadership.

You are meant to change the world, whether that's through one person or millions. And if this book can give you the inspiration, courage, or advice that helps you bring just one person closer to the Lord, then I consider it a success. From the entire Worship Online team and me, thank you for allowing us to play a small part in your journey to change the world.

How this book is formatted.

Although you're welcome to read this book from front to back, it wasn't organized that way. I invite you to skip around liberally. This book is a buffet of knowledge and inspiration. Mark sections you want to come back to, and feel free to skip sections you're not interested in. This book should be fun and inspiring to read. Start with your favorite artists, and then move to some you're not as familiar with. Treat it as your personal choose-your-own-adventure guide.

However, take a mental note of anything you didn't read so that you can return to it later. Ask yourself why you skipped that section. Was it the mentor? Was it the topic? Something said that offended you? Seemed beneath you?

I've found that taking the time to answer these questions honestly has helped me uncover blind spots or bottlenecks in my own life and ministry. Read through those sections with an open heart and open mind. Then if it still doesn't resonate, that's fine too.

What do they have in common?

Place extra importance on commonalities. One of the most exciting things you find when you organize a book like this is the common themes and advice that come up repeatedly from different people. People from different walks of life and cultures. It makes you think, if 70 to 80 percent of the most influential worship leaders in the world are saying the same thing, there must be something to it. Here are some of the common themes that kept arising during our interviews. I'm not going into detail about each here. I simply want you to take a mental note when you come across them throughout the book.

- **The power of authenticity and vulnerability.** An overwhelming number of mentors in this book talk about this—whether they're talking about vulnerability in songwriting, transparency in leading worship, or authenticity while having coffee with a friend. Allowing people to see the real you, not the pretend you, is very powerful. It gives others the freedom to be authentic as well. People that are free, free other people. Or, as I like to say, free people free people.

- **Community.** Every single mentor in this book is deeply involved in their home church communities. And 90% of them have been there for many years. In fact, I've yet to discover a song any of them has written (songs we sing every week in church) that weren't written to serve a need in their own church or community first. Your community is your tribe, your covering, your family, and the place where people know you and how to serve you. Floating around without a community is a dangerous and ineffective place to be.

- **Not being the best, but allowing God to use you.** None of the mentors here claim to be the best singers, worship leaders, or musicians. However, what's interesting is that many of them outright admit to not being great at many things. Or that when they first started, they were terrible at their craft. However, God still used them in incredible ways. We like to use the cliché that "God uses the willing," but to see these people living that out is truly inspiring. If God puts something in your heart, don't give up. This brings me to our next commonality.

- **There are no overnight successes.** I use the word "success" lightly here. Because success in the Lord can look like many different things. However, the point here is that whatever your plan is, God's is usually much different. Many of the mentors in this book took years of learning, growing, failing, and getting back up again before they ever saw what the Lord had planned for them. The journey is where God developed their hearts, which is the actual reward. Not the destination. A mentor of mine told me, "It's not about your dreams and goals. It's about the person you become on the way to those dreams and goals." So cut yourself some slack, allow yourself to "fail," and relax. Enjoy this beautiful journey.

What not to do with this book.

One of my biggest concerns in releasing a book like this is that some people will walk away thinking that to be used by God, you have to be known or famous. Or you have to look or sound a certain way. Let me be very clear. This couldn't be further from the truth.

I love how Jon Egan (Desperation Band) (Pg. 50) explained this:

> "In the Old Testament, when the people of Israel wanted a good king that was tall and handsome, they got Saul, who murdered Christians. It's similar now. We have to have our worship leaders look like secular artists or fit specific criteria. I've felt pulled into that at times, and my own insecurities began to rise up. I'd have thoughts of how I'm getting older, I'm not this articulate, or I don't look a certain way. If I can get one thing across to everyone reading this, it's that being used

by God is not dependent on your style, what you sound like, or anything other than a willing heart. Raw, real passion is so much more powerful than trying to be something you're not. We can decide that we're not going to be swept up in the scene. The presence of God carries everything, not an industry."

If there's one thing I've learned after studying our mentors in this book, it's that none of them tried to be anything that they weren't. If you want to be used by God and impact your community, you will be a lot more effective by just being who God created you to be and nothing else. If you want to be used by God, it starts in one place only, and that's your heart.

The second thing this book is not is a replacement for the Word of God. My hope is that the words of these mentors will inspire you to dive into the Word of God even more. The best we can do is provide opinions and advice that relate back to His word. But don't take anything said here as fact. I challenge you to dive into the Word of God on anything that speaks to you and see what He says about it.

1

Tasha Cobbs Leonard

Tasha Cobbs is one of the most powerful voices in music today. She's garnered multiple awards, from Grammys, Doves, and Billboard Music Awards. Her version of "Break Every Chain" landed as Billboard's #1 for 12 weeks in a row. Songs she's written include "This Is A Move," "You Know My Name," "Gracefully Broken," and many more. She's someone who models dependency on the Lord and true authority in her leadership.

IG: @TashaCobbsLeonard

tashacobbs.org

Being a late bloomer and transparency on stage.

A lot of people don't know this, but I'm what some may consider a late bloomer as it pertains to singing and leading worship. I came from a family of singers, but I didn't sing lead. I was thrust into a moment when I was 15 years old. The guy who was supposed to lead a song, "Now Behold The Lamb" by Kirk Franklin, got into a minor car accident on his way to church. At the time, I was a choir director. I didn't sing, but I knew how to direct the choir. So everybody looked at me and said, "Tasha, you've got to sing this song tonight." I had that feeling of "I don't know why y'all are looking at me." Needless to say, I sang the song that night. And when I opened my eyes, there were people crying and people kneeling in worship. I looked over at my parents, and I thought, *Wow, this is new. This is fresh.*

My father first started to cultivate the teaching and preaching gift in me when I was ten years old. And I never led a song through any of that until I was 15. So now, when I stand to minister, there's a merging of the two ministries—prophetic teaching, along with the gift of leading worship. It's something that I believe is unique about how God has called me to lead worship. I stand in the confidence of the Holy Spirit when I do that. All I have to offer is who I am. So I tell people all the time, whether I'm at the White House or standing in front of 20 people. I lead the same way. I can only be me.

It's also been effective to share personal testimonies attached to the songs I'm singing while I lead. I've seen people moved in amazing ways through me sharing stories of what I've been through and how a song or lyric helped me. There's a level of transparency there as well. A lot of people don't know that we, as worship leaders, go through moments as well. When I sing "Break Every Chain," I've had chains in my life that had to be broken, and I've experienced Jesus Christ as the chain breaker.

There's nothing wrong with practicing a spiritual moment.

When you're leading worship, knowing what to say or where to take a moment requires total dependence on Jesus Christ. It requires levels of discernment to know when to speak or when not to speak. There are moments when we are to be still in the presence of God, to hear his voice, and to hear his response. This is very practical, but practice is important for worship leaders. Practice his presence. One of my good friends, Brandon Lake, with whom I wrote the song "This Is A Move," shares a testimony about how he was just a musician for many years. He was behind the guitar and realized one day that that was his safe space. It was something that was a crutch for him. So he started rehearsing leading worship at his home without his guitar in his hand. He was practicing those moments of personal testimony and what scriptures are connected to what songs. So I would encourage worship leaders to practice those moments. It doesn't make it any less spiritual. I believe God honors our preparation.

Mentors can be people you don't know.

Mentorship is key in my life. A lot of times, people think mentors have to be touched or that they have to be somebody you can reach every single day, but I don't think that's the case. The Bible says for us to study to show ourselves approved, and that can be scripture, books, videos, etc. I study people. CeCe Winans was a mentor of mine for many years before I ever met her. I was studying her life because I loved that she walked in integrity. I loved how she loved her husband and her children. So I would encourage everyone to find a mentor. Even if it's someone you can't touch, text, or call. Find someone whose life you can study.

Diversity in ministry.

It's no secret that our world is dealing with a lot of social injustices. So, of course, a lot of eyes are on me asking, "Tasha, what are you going to say? You have access to so many people." So I'll say it this way. I believe that diversity in ministry, or reconciliation, does not start on a major platform. It starts at our dinner tables and our front doors. It starts on our phone calls and with pursuing people who don't look like you or grew up like you. Then being open to understanding their culture and what matters to them. It's about empathy. Jesus was so big on empathizing with people.

We have to show them that we are like Jesus, who loves them no matter what they're dealing with, who they are, or what they've done. That's what we are called as Christians to do. I may not agree with everything that you believe, but I love you nonetheless, and I'm going to love you even through this season of what may be extremely hard.

Alexander Pappas

Raised in Idaho and later moving to Sydney, Australia, Alexander is most widely known as a worship leader and songwriter for the twice Grammy-nominated band Hillsong Young & Free. He has led some of the biggest cries of praise and worship for the next generation, including genre-defining anthems such as "Alive," "Wake," "Real Love," and "Echo (Elevation Worship)."

IG: @alexander.pappas

alexanderpappasmusic.com

From Idaho to Sydney.

I was saved at a youth event when I was young. I remember it vividly. The band was playing Hillsong UNITED songs, and that was the first time I was amazed at the presence of God, and I related to the music and the art from those songs. When I was 17, I became the worship and band leader in our youth group in Idaho. We'd sung a couple of Hillsong UNITED songs here and there, but then the day I took over the team, my youth pastor handed me the United We Stand record. We started doing the songs from that record almost every single week.

We watched a documentary about that record, and we were shocked that they were just youth kids at a camp wanting God to use them. Our youth band was just me and two of my best friends. One kind of played the drums, and the other played trumpet. Our trumpet player was so good that he would play all of the lead guitar melodies on his trumpet. True story. Years later, I ended up in Australia, started going to church at Hillsong, and became involved in Hillsong Young & Free.

How to get team members to stick around.

Jesus is the ultimate example of what it looks like to shepherd and disciple your team. Doing this like Jesus is one of the most unbelievably admirable qualities of a pastor—people that truly carry their flock, care for them, and go after the One. The most important part of shepherding like Jesus is caring about people. I learned this the hard way. I spent my early years as a pastor saying, "Hey, I'd love to catch up. Let's talk about how you can get better at guitar. It'd be great if you watched some tutorials about getting your tone better…" As great as excellence and bringing your best in worship is, I let people down by caring more about their gift or craft than I cared about them. A good shepherd doesn't just care about the hair or the wool that can be sheared. It's not about the product; it's the value of the sheep itself. It's the value of the person.

Shifting that mentality has helped me so much as a leader. This principle applies to building teams as well. There are great churches everywhere, and people will stay where they're being shepherded. People will stay where they know they are valued, seen, and cared for. The number one thing for building a creative team is having relationships with people and caring for them as a person and not as a product.

Practical ways to organize and shepherd your team.

In a practical sense, it's the diligence of spreadsheets. Every couple of months, we'll sit down and go through the list of all the people in our database of around 500 team members and ten staff members at my campus. We'll go through the list and make sure that there is someone looking out for each person and staying in touch with them. If it's not one of the staff members, we'll see if a key leader can intentionally look out for people on their teams. It's a lot of work, but it's important work.

We do our best to have the systems in place and things like that, but I'm constantly reminded of the parable of the Sower in the Gospel of Mark. The Sower will sow the seed. Some will land on good soil, some will land on bad soil, and some will land on the gravel, spring up, and die. When it comes to what we do as leaders and believers, we are all called to sow seed. I'm encouraged to know that it's not for us to decide where the good soil is. We're just called to sow. I'm encouraged to trust God that the good seed will land where it's meant to. I just need to keep doing it. And when it comes to the even bigger picture of salvation, it's all about trusting God. It's not for me to decide which soil is which. He's doing the work in the soil. He's doing the work of the unseen. All I need to work on is what's seen.

3

Jake France

Jake is a worship leader, musician, and songwriter. He's currently the worship pastor at Harvest Bible Chapel in Chicago, but you may know him from his six years of leading worship as part of Vertical Worship.

IG @jakefrance21

Why the Lord won't bless your church's album.

Whenever people see Vertical Worship and the songs that are just now starting to get popular, like our song, "Yes I Will," you don't realize that that's just the tip of the iceberg of what God has been doing at this church long before I ever showed up. My church now, Harvest, has been making records for almost 30 years and has an endless catalog of songs and albums. And for any worship leaders, or anyone writing songs, there has to be a giant avalanche of ice underneath the water before you ever see the iceberg and the fruit of the harvest. It requires a lot of work, energy, and a lot of time spent in a secret place with God getting to know his heart. If your motivation is to write and create an album so that these songs get popular, the Lord's not going to bless that. You can't fake intimacy.

Write a lot, and get ready for feedback.

If you want to start a songwriting culture at your church, you need to be extremely open and ready to receive feedback. I think it's really easy to sit down and write a song, but it's really hard to sit down and write a good song. Obviously, songwriting, like any art form, is extremely subjective, but a good litmus test is just to see if there are people reacting to the songs that you're writing. If they're putting their weight behind it and standing up and saying, "Wow, this song has something anointed on it," or "This song could really bless this person," those are good indicators. So, a very important first step is to start getting your songs around a lot of people. Every time we go into a record cycle, we write around a hundred songs that we have to narrow down to ten or eleven. And those songs are chosen based on what people are reacting to the most.

The rules of songwriting sessions.

We have some rules that we bring into our songwriting sessions that keep the creativity flowing. The biggest rule that we have is that you can't say "no" to anyone's idea whenever you're in the writing room. You can only add a "yes" to someone's idea. For instance, if I come up with a line and the other people that I'm writing with aren't a fan of it, they aren't allowed to say they don't like it. They're only allowed to add their own idea to it. This way, we keep bouncing ideas around and off of each other until the end result is something great. Nothing kills creativity faster than negativity.

However, once the song is written, you've got demo number one done, and you're in the editing room, that's when you can be critical. Let's nitpick and get the best version of the song possible. We also write in groups of three. We've found that that's the sweet spot for keeping things moving forward throughout the session. You could have two people that may be kind of brain dead in the moment but still have someone else churning out ideas that keep things flowing.

Collaborating with other churches in your community.

Even if you're thinking, "Well, you don't know how small my team is," or "I don't have anyone to write with," there are other churches and worship pastors in your community that would probably be dying to get together with you and write a song. Think about how multiple churches singing this one original song could transform a city or town. That is so exciting to me. It's so easy for that to happen, too. Just pick up the phone and call someone, even if you don't know them, and say, "Hey, I'm the worship pastor at this church down the road. I'm trying to write some songs for my church, and I don't have anyone to write with." You'll just be amazed by what the Lord does through that because the Lord loves collaboration.

Deciding who on the team gets to be part of the album.

You can look around and see this being done in such an unhealthy way on both extremes. Some churches keep such a small team that everyone feels left out. And at the other end spectrum, some churches try to get everyone involved so that no one feels left out. This is a leadership question and a leadership issue more than anything else. The win is to try and get as many people involved as possible, but knowing that you have to draw the line at some point. However, I would make sure that whenever you're making decisions about who sings or does what, you're not the only person making them. There needs to be some sort of committee making those decisions. I think there are ways to get creative. For example, have a choir off to the side of the stage that will sing all the crowd vocals so you can get more people involved and things like that.

Advice to new worship leaders/musicians.

Serve and serve for free. There are a lot of subsets of our culture that pay their musicians, which I think is great. But for a young worship team member, don't think that you deserve to get paid every single time you get up on stage. There's an obvious blessing that happens whenever you give your time and talent to the Lord. Serve as much as you possibly can, especially if you're young. You have way more time than you think you have right now, and you should be on stage as much as you possibly can.

4

Phil Joel

Phil Joel is a multi-talented musician, worship leader, and songwriter. He's known for his solo work, being the founder of the worship band Zealand, as well as being the bass player and vocalist for Newsboys.

zealand.band

Growing up on the road with Newsboys and getting injured.

I've been full-time with Newsboys for over 13 years. I basically grew up in the band. It's funny because I can just look across the stage and see Jody. He taught me how to shave. And there's Dunkin; we were all at each other's weddings. And then there's Peter. I think he was the first guy to hold my baby other than my wife and me. We've done real life together. And there we are on stage in these arenas just doing what we do. It's natural and easy. Although these days my body doesn't enjoy it much anymore because there's a lot of jumping. On the third show of the most recent tour, I was jumping around having a blast, and I tore a muscle. It just about destroyed me.

Which style of worship music is best?

As someone who's been involved in worship music for most of my life, I've seen different styles of worship music come and go. Don't get hung up on the style because you know what? We're all worshiping. We're just doing it differently. Everyone has grown up differently, during different times, listening to different genres, going to church, or not going to church. Some hearts resonate with different sounds, different chord combinations, or different lyrics. Maybe someone hasn't grown up in church, so certain statements and phrases don't make any sense to that person. But there are styles of music that will open different people's hearts. So that's why

I would encourage everyone to continue creating new styles of music and experimenting with sounds and combinations. No style is better than another, just different. And there's room for us all at the table: pop, indie, alternative, rap, and whatever gets invented in the future.

Early on in the days of Zealand, I started hearing things from people saying that we were trying to jump on the worship bandwagon. And my response to that was, "What do you think I've been doing for 25 years?" Whether it's a rock song, a pop song, or whatever, we've always tried to remind people of who God is, his goodness, and his grace. The style of music doesn't matter as much.

What is worship to you?

Worship is about remembering. However, God doesn't forget who He is. We forget who He is. So we show up on Sunday to remember. We can relax and say, "Yes, I remember again. You're God. I'm not. You're faithful. I'm kind of marginally faithful at different points. You are good, and you have good things for your kids. I can trust you. Yeah. I remember now." Then we breathe deep, and we walk out of that place, standing a little bit taller and ready to carry that worship throughout the week.

Finding your own sound.

The record we just put out is called "Liberated." The ironic thing is that at a certain point in the process, I found myself being liberated as well. I was trying to make a record that I wasn't meant to make. I was trying to write songs I wasn't meant to write, and we ended up with a full record. I had to sit back and go, "It's not right." The record company loved me (sarcasm). I had to go to them and say, "Hey, this isn't correct. I'm really sorry."

Within the "worship genre," there are certain marks you have to hit for these songs to be sung in the church. And I get it, some people are just built to write songs for the church, and that's their mission, their vision, and that's what they do. They are brilliant at it, but if they step outside of that, they struggle. For me, I made this record with the guys, and we just had to say, "Nope, it's not who we are." We've got new songs that we need to record, and we need to get rid of some of the other ones. It's so important to have the courage to be who you are and not try to be just like Jesus Culture, Bethel, or Hillsong. You just be you. Which is easier said than done. It's easy just to be someone else, but we should all be scratching and clawing for expressions that come from our own hearts. So we trashed some songs, went back, and made the record we needed to make, not the one we were supposed to make.

Why he and his band members don't use social media.

One of the big things that we don't do as a band is social media. We just don't do it. We believe that it takes more than it gives and dilutes real relationships and authentic connections with people and God. We're all looking for the same three things. We want to be seen, understood, and liked. We're born with that, and I think that's okay. God's put that in us because he's the only one that can fulfill it. We've gotta get that from Him. We have to understand that He sees us, understands us, and He actually likes us.

As we get ourselves full on that, then we can give, too. But if we're trying to get that from other avenues, they just end up taking, over-promising, and under-delivering. Then we end up breathing shallowly. As a band, it's kind of a little flag we wave and say, "Hey, you don't have to do some of the things that you feel culture telling you to do." Our fear is that we're gonna lose touch or something, but the Bible says, "What good is it if you gain the whole world, but lose your soul?" That's a big thing these days. We're becoming soulless in a lot of ways because we're not connecting with God and with one another in real, rich, true, authentic ways. That's my soapbox for the day.

Best advice for worship leaders/musicians.

Being teachable is the most important factor when it comes to honing your craft. I can take someone who's been playing an instrument or singing for years, who isn't teachable, and put them up against someone new who is willing, hungry to learn, and quick to make adjustments. It'll only be a matter of time before the new person is more skilled than the "veteran."

Second, someone said to me one time, "If you're the most talented guy in the room, you're in the wrong room." So surround yourself and cozy up with people who are doing what you want to do and learn, observe, and ask questions. Don't be afraid or too prideful to ask questions; I personally love it when people ask me for advice or how I did something.

So, to sum it up, be teachable and be curious.

5

Jon Egan

Jon Egan is a worship leader and songwriter who's been serving at New Life Church in Colorado Springs for over 18 years. He's one of the founders of Desperation Conference as well as Desperation Band and has written many songs that churches sing every single week, such as "My Savior Lives," "Overcome," "I Am Free," and "Here In Your Presence." He has collaborated with top Christian writers, producers, and artists, including Jason Ingram, Paul Mabury, Mia Fieldes, Jeremy Camp, Kari Jobe, and Paul Baloche.

IG: @joncegan

God is going to do what he wants to do. Even if you don't have talent.

I grew up playing drums in my church until my dad sent me an album by this new band called "Delirious". There was something about not only the way Martin Smith wrote songs but the way he delivered them. It really spoke to me, and that's when I decided that it was time to get off the drums and time to lead and sing. However, I didn't even know if I could. And it turned out that I really couldn't. I was quite bad, but I just kept at it.

I started leading worship late in college, and again, I wasn't very good. I only knew four chords on the guitar and had no singing ability. Around that time, some friends of mine called and said, "Hey, we're looking for someone to come and lead worship for the youth group at church every week." That church was New Life, which I've now been a part of for over 18 years. Pretty soon after that, one of our youth pastors, David Perkins, told me they were going to start a worship and prayer gathering called Desperation, and he wanted me to lead worship for it along with some other guys. Of course, I said yes, but I was also wondering, "Are you sure you want me to do it?" He also knew some guys at the church that knew how to record, so on top of leading, he wanted me to write some songs to record an album. I had never written a song before.

At the time, I was really green and thrust into this new world so fast. I really had no business doing any of it when it came to just my gifting and talent. However, I've found that God is going to do what he wants to do with who he wants to do it with. I just got to be in the swirl of all that. So from there, we just started writing songs for our youth group and our church, which turned into the Desperation Band and Desperation Conference.

Clinging to God during criticism.

That was now 18 years ago, and I'll be 40 in two weeks. However, after everything that I've seen God do, I still struggle with rather having certainty over faith. Every day, you have to lean into Jesus and decide you're either gonna go for it, or you're gonna sit this one out. I decided I was gonna go for it. And with that, there's no promise that you won't feel the hits and the criticism because it came. We heard things like we're too young, don't know how to sing, or can't do this or that thing right. There were times when I remember licking our wounds, wanting just to forget the whole thing. I felt like we were wrong, they were right, and we shouldn't have done this.

However, in the book of Jeremiah, he talks about how he is feeling the heat. What he needs to be doing is like a fire that shot up in his bones. He needs to get this out, or he'll explode. And I resonated with that. I had to do this. When it comes down to it, you have to be obedient. You have just to keep going. God, you're with me, so here we go.

Worship keeps us going.

Worship has been the thing that has made me last. I'm a passionate worship leader because the presence of God is this place of incredible safety and breakthrough. I've seen the most breakthrough in my life through declaring the realities of God through worship. We go through things in life that are very real, like fear, sickness, or death. But when we worship God, we start declaring things that stand in full opposition to fear, sickness, death, and anything else the enemy throws at us. The realities of God stand in opposition to our earthly realities, and all of a sudden, our earthly realities grow dim.

You don't have to be famous to be used by God.

One of my deepest concerns and burdens for young people coming up is that they look at the worship scene and mistakenly think that being used by God means that you have to be known and famous. Or they think you have to look a certain way or sound a certain way. That is such a lie from Hell. You can see it with social media and how it's presenting this picture of what it looks like to be used by God. And unless we dig deeper, we're going to think that we have to be this specific thing to reach people.

In the Old Testament, when the people of Israel wanted a king that was tall and handsome, they got Saul, who murdered Christians. It's similar now. We have to have our worship leaders look like secular artists or fit certain criteria. I've felt pulled into that at times, and my own insecurities began to show. I'd have thoughts of how I'm getting older, I'm not this articulate, or I don't look a certain way. If I can get one thing across to everyone reading this, it's that being used by God is not dependent on your style, what you sound like, or anything other than a willing heart. Raw, real passion is so much more powerful than trying to be something you're not. We can decide that we're not going to be swept up in the scene. The presence of God carries everything, not an industry. And I hope people my own age, who've come up through it and may be jaded, could remember their first love and why they started doing this in the first place.

Phil Thompson
—

It wasn't until he was 30 years old that Phil Thompson discovered his gift for writing music. Not only did he establish himself as the writer behind Ashmont Hill's hits, but he's also inked songs for a multitude of artists, most notably JJ Hairston's "Love Lifted Me". His live worship session "My Worship" gained over 12 million views within a year of its release. The full project was released in Spring 2018 and reached #1 on the Billboard charts. It garnered both Dove Awards and Stellar Awards nominations. Within the year, Phil has crisscrossed the globe, worshiping throughout Ghana, Nigeria, the United Kingdom, the Netherlands, Canada and the Caribbean Islands.

IG: @philthompsonworship

philthompsonworship.com

"I will never lead worship. I'm too shy for that." A message to the introverts.

Many people don't know this, but when I started to be involved in music, I wanted to stay in the background. On the day of recording for the worship album "My Worship" that I had written, I had somebody else lined up to lead the whole thing. I was supposed to be in the back singing back-up. I didn't want to lead because I didn't feel like I could do it justice. But before the recording, I had two different people back out on me who were supposed to lead. I couldn't cancel because the studio session was already booked, and people were coming to record the audio and video. So in the ninth hour, I recorded it because I had to. That's how I started out leading worship.

I was forced to step out front. I was the writer, and I was happy just being in the background singing back-up. I've since learned and grown to have the confidence to lead, but I used to look at people leading worship and think to myself, *Oh my God, I would never be able to do that. There's just such confidence they have in the way that they command the stage.* My brother had been asking me for years, "Phil, I want you to lead worship." And I remember telling him, "You'll never see me on stage leading worship. That will never happen." I was just too shy for that. When Seinfeld said that death was only the number two biggest fear for people, and public speaking was number one, I related with that.

One day, when I was a background singer, the person leading prayed this prayer, "Lord, take center stage so that you would be seen and so that you would be glorified." That prayer penetrated me. It quickly became my mantra. Worship became not about me anymore because the Lord takes center stage. Now I feel that if I ever try to lead worship and I don't ask Him to take center stage, it's going to unveil me as this big fraud. Once He takes center stage, it's all about Him. I can step off to the side and just allow God to do what he does.

My number one piece of advice to anyone out there that's like me and naturally introverted or shy would be not to try and be something you're not. Everything that we do should come from a place of authenticity. Every song that you sing, let that song touch your life. Allow it to be deeply connected to you so that way, when you stand up and sing that song, people feel it. It's not about how much stage presence you have. Sure, stage presence helps, but it's not about that. It's certainly not about how great you can sing because some of my favorite worship leaders that I've ever seen over the years are not singers. It's about your heart and being authentically connected to what you're saying. Remembering that will alleviate the pressure of you trying to showcase anything. If it's authentic, the people will feel it. If you're connected to it, you'll be able to communicate it more strongly. There are people in the congregation who will resonate with the screamers, and there are people who will resonate with the quietest and most intimate. You be you.

A message to those who don't know what they want to do in life.

We tend to think that not knowing every detail of our lives is a bad thing. I heard Tasha Cobbs talk about living her life in the fog and becoming comfortable with that. When you're in a fog, you don't know exactly where you're heading, and you can only see what's immediately in front of you. When you're walking with God, sometimes that's what it is. I would never have guessed that I would be walking the path that I'm walking right now with the confidence that I have. I know that I'm exactly where the Lord wants me to be. I would've never guessed that this would be my lane. I was a philosophy major that became a gym teacher, became a songwriter that became a recording artist. And through all of that, I'm learning to become comfortable in the fog and not knowing what the next step is. I can look back now from my vantage point and see all the little dots that connected. However, in the midst of it, I was full of anxiety, not knowing where I was going. That's why faith is the most amazing part of my life. I'm dependent on God for whatever this next step or season is.

7

Josh Miller

Josh Miller is a worship leader who heads up the worship teams at Saddleback Church, in which Rick Warren is the pastor. Saddleback Church is a massive organization with 18 campuses, so Josh is an expert at systems and processes that only enhance what God is doing, not take away from it.

IG: @joshua_david_m

Over-communication is how we love our team.

I grew up in a church of 70 to 80 people, so when I came to Saddleback, it was such a shift for me in not only size but in the complexity of how the church operates. However, our worship pastor, John Cassetto's vision for the team has always been First Corinthians 14: "Let love be your highest goal." So we may be a big church with a big team, but at the center of our team is love and family. You can see it when you go places where the team hangs out. We have our families there and kids running around. You can feel it because our intention as a team is to have love above everything else. That's the banner over our team and how we operate.

With that said, as a team with many members and services each week, we have to have deep processes. And those processes start with communication. One of the things we talk about on the team is that communication is how we love each other. An example of one of these communication processes is that we create these documents called "song scans." It's one of the coolest ways to love production people by letting them know the details of the arrangement and flow of the service so that they're not guessing. Anything can happen in the service, but we give them a skeleton of the plan.

The document shows the lyrics, where the instrumentals are, the ebb and flow of the service, and a rundown of how the service will go. The best way we can love the production team is by communicating what we're going to do ahead of time in the week. You'd be surprised at how helpful it is. The only way to break something really complex into digestible pieces is to over-communicate and make it as simple as you can.

Specific things you can do right now to encourage your team.

There have been some habits over the years that I've had to break. One of them is the habit of only reaching out to people and checking in on them if they are scheduled to be part of the service. I made the decision very early on that I was always going to find people to reach out to and check in on, especially if it was a week that I wasn't going to need them. I'll just look at our planning center to see who's not scheduled and check in on them, so they know that I'm not only checking in on them because I need something from them. The quickest thing that will burn a volunteer out is if they feel like they're being used.

I'm a task person. I love lists and like getting things done. I'm sure there are a lot of leaders who can relate to that. But at the end of the day, God cares about his people. Yes, he cares about the fruits of what we do, and he cares about excellence, but above all, he cares about people. And if he cares about people and is willing to stop and pray for the sick, or stop and be interrupted to focus on the one, then we can do that as well. It's much easier said than done because we have so many tasks and things we want to accomplish, but people are always the priority. We have to keep reminding ourselves of that.

Another thing that motivates and empowers people is making sure that everything we do has a vision behind it. We always take a moment to pause and focus on God somehow, whether that's through prayer, testimony, or a word. If we're going from service to service, mid-week conference, a night of worship, album recording, or whatever it is, and there's no vision behind it, then what's the point? If there's not a solid word and direction, then we're just mindlessly going on stage and doing whatever we're doing. Vision, purpose, and meaning are what empower people to go the extra mile. Without that purpose, people lose passion and get burned out. So we constantly have to keep reminding ourselves of why we're doing what we're doing.

Jared Runion & Emily Wyant
—

Jared and Emily are members of the band Local Sound. Local Sound is a movement born from within the Nashville-based college ministry, MyLocal. They see themselves as culture creators who support the work of the local church in the lives of young adults. As a new band, their fresh sound spreads like wildfire as they have already toured with Mosaic MSC, Cody Carnes, Mack Brock, and more to come.

IG: @localsound

localsoundband.com

Emily – Finding your purpose.

One of the biggest realizations I've had in the last year was when Jesus said, "I came so you can have life and life abundantly." Don't get me wrong, excellence is important, but sometimes we get so caught up in goals, achievements, direction, and hustle that we don't realize that we already have everything we need to represent the specific portion of the Lord's heart that we have been called to represent. For example, the Lord has called me to represent joy in every conversation and interaction I have with people. Your portion of the Lord's heart may be graciousness, peace, justice, or anything that brings light to the world. When you realize that everyone is representing a different piece of the Lord's heart, you can see that we each have a specific calling and purpose.

That realization gives you grace for others and allows you to love them better. When I represent joy, I do it boldly. However, I don't expect that same level of joy from others. I have my thing, and they have theirs. We are the body of Christ working together in a unique way. There's a confidence you gain when you realize the part of God's heart that you're representing. You can be yourself to the best of your ability, and all this comparing yourself to others goes out the window.

Jared – Church music doesn't suck.

God is doing something brand new in the church, and it's a big weighty thing that young people are being called into.

There's an obstacle, though. Our obstacle is getting this honor thing right. If we don't, we're going to have a much more difficult time doing the things that God's calling us to do. For instance, I can't hear any more young worship leaders talk about how crappy church music is. That is such a dishonorable thing to say. Take, for example, the song "Open The Eyes Of My Heart." That song was a bridge to move my Baptist church from hymns to modern church music. What I'm saying is that the people from the nineties and the early two thousands made music that paved the way for us to make the music that we're making today.

This idea that they got it wrong and we're about to get it right is garbage. God is much bigger than that. When God introduces Himself as the God of Abraham, Isaac, and Jacob, he's saying that he's much bigger than just your short years. He's unrolling a story of redemption from generation to generation. Can we just take a moment to honor those who had gone before us in the faith and say thank you for being faithful when it wasn't easy all the time? Take Paul Baloche and Darlene Zschech. They had struggles, but they rolled up their sleeves and wrote with all the faith they had for their churches. And that has absolutely paved the way for us to do what we're doing today.

Rita Springer

Rita Springer is a worship leader and songwriter who's been releasing albums for the church for over 26 years. In that time, she's released 12 albums. She's also known for being a worship leader at Gateway Church. Songs she's written include "Stand In Your Love," "Defender," and "Never Lost."

IG: @RitaSpringer

ritaspringer.com

Being 55 with the energy of a 20-year-old and creating new sounds.

What's really important for people to understand—young and old—is that when you truly have an encounter with the Lord and want to be in ministry, you have to see yourself as a progressive, pertaining to where the Lord wants to take you. Too many leaders are only in something until it no longer validates them, or they get past the age of what others tell them is viable for certain things. The age thing has always been in the back of my head. However, in my journey with the Lord, He said, "Greater the things you'll do in the latter part of your life than ever the former" (Haggai 2:9).

I really grabbed a hold of that. I've remained in this progressive state of receiving fresh ideas, a newer vision, and better dreams. You don't get old to stop doing those things. You get old to flourish. So, in this journey with the Lord, I keep receiving new ideas. We started a women's ministry, we've been doing conferences, and we've also started a school of ministry.

On top of that, I'm still releasing albums and writing books. I never thought I'd be one with so many ideas, but the older I get, the more the Lord keeps wanting to give me more. Just because we're vessels that get older doesn't mean that we don't get wiser. In that wisdom, we grab a hold of the next thing God's wanting for us to do. I don't think God wants us just to get a camper and retire. I don't want to go camping; I feel like God's given me something to do. My ear is pressed to the heart of the Lord, always asking, "What's next?"

I'm probably one of the oldest worship leaders around. However, it's funny that the majority of my listeners are in their twenties and thirties. They're not in my age bracket. So that's saying something about the music that God is creating through me. I'll ask God questions, and He says, "Nope, we're not making music that is from your decade. I want to hear new sounds. I want to give you fresh sounds." So I'm always chasing down beautiful new melody lines, and I have a knack for finding them because I'm confident they can be found because God told me they were there.

10

Krissy Nordhoff

—

Krissy Nordhoff is a Grammy-nominated, Dove Award-winning songwriter. Her songs have been recorded by artists such as Tauren Wells, Jenn Johnson, Natalie Grant, Mandisa, Darlene Zschech, Aaron Shust, Anthony Evans, Meredith Andrews, Todd Agnew, Phillips, Craig & Dean, Corey Voss, and plenty more. Krissy is also the founder of BRAVE WORSHIP and the author of Writing Worship: How to Craft Heartfelt Songs for the Church.

IG: @krissy_nordhoff

krissynordhoff.com

Two exercises to do every day before writing songs.

Two spiritual exercises that I do every day are "Two-Way Journaling" and "Psalming." I used to always talk to the Lord when I would pray, but I didn't necessarily always stop and listen for him to speak back to me. Two-Way Journaling is when you journal your prayers, your thoughts, and your feelings. Sometimes it's a verse or a specific word that the Lord's highlighting to you out of scripture. Once you've written it out in your journey, it's time to let Him guide you. You start to listen and let Him speak, and as He does, you write what He says to you.

Psalming is just singing the Psalms out loud. I can't tell you how many of the worship songs I've written were birthed from just singing through the Psalms. Doing these two things really helps prepare my heart as I go into writing sessions. If you just get into that place of true worship, when you're by yourself with the Lord, you can take that with you, whether leading worship or writing in a room.

If you have a need, become what you need for others.

My sister and I do a ministry together called Brave Worship. For the first 15 years I was in Nashville, I had been praying for a mentor. At the end of year 15, I said, "Lord, why have you not answered that prayer?" I couldn't find anybody who was a female in the music industry and juggled family and ministry the same way I was. He basically said, "Be what you need." So, around ten years ago, I began gathering girls in my living room. My sister saw the need for mentoring females in the worship-leading arena, and I saw the need on the songwriting side. We decided to partner up so we could reach a broader audience of girls. Now we have a podcast, a course, and we do local events.

We want to encourage the voice of the female. It's crazy, but if you look at the numbers in the US church, about 75% are female. And about 80% of what's being written in Christian music is being written by men. A lot of times, women feel like they're disqualified once they have kids, and that's just not the case. You're not giving up your dreams by having children. You actually now have an even bigger responsibility because now you're a role model. They're watching you and learning from you.

Starting this ministry switched my frame of mind from one of taking to one of giving. Through this process, I found community, and it's probably the healthiest thing I've been a part of. It's been a very non-competitive environment, which is hard to find in the creative world, and it's been a place of encouraging and championing each other. Experiencing need gives you the wisdom for how to meet a need. Because who better to create something to meet the needs of others than someone who has gone through needing that thing themselves? If you never experienced the need, you wouldn't know how to give.

11

William McDowell

An acclaimed pastor and worship leader, William McDowell is known for his exuberant, contemporary praise and worship albums. Based out of Orlando's Deeper Fellowship Church, McDowell first gained wide attention with 2009's number three Billboard Gospel Album "As We Worship Live." He has remained a chart regular, issuing top-ten albums like "Arise: The Live Worship Experience," the Dove Award-winning "Sounds of Revival," and "The Cry: A Live Worship Experience."

IG: @pastorwilliammcdowell

williammcdowellmusic.com

Self-exaltation vs. self-denial.

One of the highest forms of worship is self-denial. If you look at what took place in the garden, Adam and Eve were made in the image and likeness of God. The serpent tempts them by saying, "The Lord knows that those who eat of this tree will be just like God." Well, Adam and Eve were already like God in his image and likeness. So what the serpent was actually tempting them with was that they will be like God because they will receive what God receives. The one thing that God received that they did not was worship. Creation was subject to Adam and Eve, but creation did not have to worship them.

Adam and Eve were reaching for equality with God and to be worshiped. They were reaching for the exaltation of self. Today we call that celebrity. As men, we're not built for fame. We're not built to handle fame and celebrity. Our crowns are to be cast, and our lives are to be laid down. The reality of worship is that self-denial and self-exaltation cannot coexist. So you're going to have to choose which one it's going to be for you. It's either about Him or it's about you, but it's not about both.

Proper worship kills the desire to be worshiped. If that desire exists in you, or any desire that doesn't give God glory, the only way to crucify that desire is to acknowledge that there's one greater than you so that you lay down all things at his feet. Jesus says to "take up your cross daily and follow me." The wording there says "daily." You must lay down your desires daily and on a recurring basis. You can spend forty years building a reputation and destroy it in forty seconds. It's the same thing as it relates to your walk with God; just because you were good doesn't mean you are good. We have to crucify our desires daily.

The two most important qualities of a leader.

Sometimes I get asked how I lead those underneath me or a variation of that question. I always have to stop and point out that you've already got it wrong if you're asking that question. There's a keyword that we have to switch in those questions. First, no one is "underneath" us, or beneath us, or below us. When we look at the model of Jesus in the book of John, the scripture talks about this moment where Jesus recognized that the Father had put all things under his control and under his power. Well, the first thing Jesus does is get up from the table and wash the feet of his disciples. The example that he gave in that moment was that the greatest of all is going to be a servant. Ephesians tells us that "he gave the apostles, the prophets, the evangelists, the shepherds and teachers, to equip the saints for the work of ministry, for building up the body of Christ."

The goal of those gifts that were given to the church was for the equipping of the saints. This means that our position by nature is a position of serving and equipping others. One of the great challenges, particularly of the American believer, is to take a capitalistic mindset in Christianity, which is to say that my vision is served by other people. However, the kingdom operates differently. The kingdom mindset says that I serve God's vision and equip his people, which also means that I am the least or the servant of all. The kingdom mindset says that even if you're a leader, you're a servant. And that servant heart must be in your posture and everything you do.

Secondly, one of the things that we've not necessarily done a good job with, in all circles, is understanding the relational equity of having people in your life who can speak to you. If everyone around you is under you, you have a problem. The mindset of eldership in scripture is that we are co-equals. Paul was able to challenge Peter, even though Paul didn't initially walk with the twelve disciples. He was able to challenge Peter because there was a recognition of their equality. We see this in Galatians when there was a disagreement between the Jerusalem church and the Antioch church.

If no one in your life can challenge you where you are or tell you, "Hey, you are wrong," then you will fall. You're gonna walk in some level of pride. There has to be a level of relationship in your life where people are not necessarily under you. One of the things that we see as a great challenge for many leaders is that no one in their immediate circle can challenge or speak to them. God uses community to work out sanctification in you. There are parts of you that you cannot see on your own. God puts you in community in order to work out the parts of you that are not good. So just to recap, first, there's a mindset shift that has to take place, which is that if you're going to lead or be in a position that's considered to be elevated, you are a servant. And the second thing is that you have to have people in your world that are not under you but are equal to you that God can use to sharpen you.

12

Meredith Andrews

Meredith Andrews is a worship leader and songwriter who was previously part of the Vertical Worship team. She now leads regularly at her home church, The Belonging Co., in Nashville, TN. She has been a part of multiple songs sung by churches across America, such as "Open Up The Heavens," "Lamb of God," "Not For A Moment," and "Spirit of the Living God." She has also garnered two Dove Awards.

IG: @meremusic

meredithandrews.com

Leading worship when you don't feel like it.

I find that when I've had a rough day, or on days when it's obvious that my family or I are under some sort of spiritual attack, those are the days when I step into worship in even a greater way. I may not want to, but once I press through, God always finds me when I need him most. I also realize that worship is warfare. I'm not going to allow my circumstances to steal my worship because God is bigger than all of that, and he's still worthy. When you press into worship when you don't necessarily feel like it, you begin to get to a place of victory and to a place where you're singing truth over your heart and over the people. You start with declaring what is true, even if you can't physically see it at the moment.

Worship takes you above your circumstances. Praise precedes our miracle, but so often, we wait until everything in our life lines up before we give God our praise. However, he's always worthy whether we're in the valley or on the mountain. I've found that worship has become a tool of warfare and intercession. We're on the front lines, and the enemy has no authority. So, I'm going to go after God with all I've got and watch those walls fall down, strongholds be rooted out, and things come into alignment as I align my heart with who God is and what He says.

Your surrender leads the way for others.

About a week before we recorded our live album, we were experiencing all kinds of opposition and attack. Anything you can think of against our family or our health was swirling around us. I remember leading worship at church while being broken and desperate for God. So much so that I was weeping and couldn't sing. I was trying to sing but just couldn't. As we went into the song "I love you, Lord," I literally couldn't get the words out. However, it became the sweetest moment between me and God. I came to a place where I didn't care what happened with the recording. I wanted Him to strip everything away so that I could make a sweet sound in His ears. I got to a place of raw, vulnerable surrender.

That night, talking to people afterward, I was continuously told of how my surrender had laid the groundwork for them to go to a place of surrender themselves. I learned an important lesson as a worship leader. We don't have to have it all together, try to save face, or hide the emotion of everything. We can just rip the bandaid off and show exactly where we are coming from. We can show that this is the situation we're walking through, but we're going to sing into it, sing over it, and declare what's true. We can come with complete surrender and give God access to the good, the bad, the ugly, the hard, and everything else. It's all his.

It unlocks something in the room and in people. I used to think that I had to make sure everybody was with me when I led. Or that I had to be aware of everything that was going on in the room. As worship leaders, it is part of our responsibility not to leave anyone behind, so for instance, the person on the back row doesn't feel like they're far away or missing out.

However, I do believe that there's something so genuine when you let it all out and go after God. Then invite everyone to come with you. Some of the moments when I encountered God the most didn't happen because someone was prodding me. It was because they were going after God the best way they knew how, with total abandon—so much that I couldn't help but want to follow right into that.

13

Katelyn Hill
—

Katelyn Hill is an incredibly gifted worship leader and songwriter with the heart of a pastor. She studied Worship and Artist Development at Liberty University while singing for their campus band. After college, she served as the Worship Pastor at Journey Church in Nashville, TN, and led a team of influential worship leaders and Grammy-winning recording artists and songwriters.

IG: @katevhill_katevhill.com

There's room at the table for you.

While I was studying worship at Liberty University, I got an opportunity to do an internship at Journey Church in Nashville, TN. A part of me was hesitant to do an internship in Nashville because I was intimidated by how many amazing musicians and vocalists lived there. I thought, "Why would I go there? There are already so many amazing people there with similar gifts. What if I can't contribute?" Despite all of the fears and insecurities, I decided to accept the internship. After I finished college, I accepted a job offer from the church and moved to Nashville.

In Nashville, it's easy to be intimidated because there are so many talented people around you with unique yet similar gifts. On top of that, Journey Church is a unique place because there are multiple worship recording artists that serve on the worship team and several other artists that attend the church with their families. Being surrounded by so many incredible musicians and artists, I had to continually fight comparison. The Lord taught me the value of diving into community and sharing hearts with people, and not letting my gift be the focus. I discovered that there was room at the table for everyone in God's plan. God creates space for each of us and invites us to join Him in creating belonging for other people.

The ugly side of comparison.

Comparison is always going to skew your perspective. It's never going to put you in a position of seeing the truth or seeing reality through a lens of love. It puts you in a position of fear. When I've given into comparison, I've seen two things happen in my own life:

- 1. You try to get big, puff up your ego, or prove yourself. And you try to defend yourself with self-promotion.
- 2. You're tempted to get really small, shrink back, and hide. You'll try to convince yourself why God can't use you and why you don't deserve to be there with your other brothers and sisters in the kingdom.

I've wrestled with comparison all throughout my life, and both of these options feel gross. When I feel tempted to get big, it almost feels holier to get small. It feels holier to talk myself out of why I can do this, but that is not how we should see ourselves as children of God.

Practical tips for finding freedom from comparison.

Worship leading is an interesting thing because it's our artistry, our craft, and our expression. However, at the same time, it's pastoring and reading the room. We want to be in a posture that allows for people to be invited into God's presence. It's the paradox of being seen so that you can be out of the way. To be a healthy worship leader, we have to spend time alone with God and ask, "What does leading worship look like for me in my story? How do I show up in my fullness without apologizing but also remain in the posture of bringing others with me by championing and encouraging them?" I think that's where real freedom happens.

We have to be very proactive when we are faced with comparison. You can't be passive. We have to bring these feelings to the Lord because fear falls away in the face of Jesus and the face of truth. One practical thing that I do a lot is journaling. I write out what I'm thankful for and what God's doing in my life. It's so important to remind yourself of your history with God and where he's brought you. I'll write something down like, "God, you've been so good to me. I'm so blessed to be with these people and get to do this." Comparison is a scarcity mindset. It causes you to be afraid that someone else's abundance might lead to your own scarcity. In reality, these things have nothing to do with each other.

Another practical way of finding freedom from comparison is through confession. When we're alone, it's easy to hide and wallow in our insecurities, but it's so important to be honest and vulnerable with your community. We all need safe people around us that we can trust. You don't want to feed off of each other's insecurities, so you need people in your life that will point you back to the truth and help you become more realigned with who God says you are.

Confession brings things into the light. It's something that I've done with my mentors and leaders. I need to work this out because I don't want to get in the way of what God's doing and how he's using me. I don't want to be afraid to empower this person whom I'm intimidated by. Sometimes you have to act before you feel it. You have to take the steps to either stand up and lead, or if you feel your ego swelling up, humble yourself, empower someone else, and cheer them on.

14

Kim Walker-Smith

Kim Walker-Smith is a worship leader and songwriter best known for her part in the band Jesus Culture as well as being a worship pastor for Bethel Church in Redding, CA. Her version of "How He Loves" has been viewed over 22 million times on YouTube. She's written countless worship songs, including "Alive In You," "Love Has A Name," and "Show Me Your Glory."

IG: @KimWalkerSmith

How to not be a passive Christian.

It's very easy to feel like you have a good relationship with God because you go to church on Sunday, sing songs, listen to the word, and have a good time. But a relationship with God is much more than that. A relationship with God is connecting to his heart daily and recognizing when that connection is lacking. I compare this daily journey to connect with God to a fight because we have life, stress, families, bills, jobs, no job, or whatever it is all trying to come in and pull our attention or pull on our anxiety. However, when we fight daily for that connection, God becomes so close that none of these external things can sway us, pull us away, or take away our faith. It can be easy sometimes to get really comfortable and be a passive Christian.

Life with Christ is not a passive thing. A life with Christ is intentional and constantly moving toward, and fighting, for that relationship. For those who are married, you understand this in a different way. You can't say you have a great marriage just because every night you sit down to dinner, raise the kids in agreement, and don't fight. If you're never intentional with each other, take the time to have a date night, or have intentional conversations, your marriage would be very lacking because you're not nurturing your connection. To have a nurtured connection to the Lord requires us to be intentional in our religion.

Some personality types make it hard to surrender.

I sometimes have a tendency to think that since I surrendered my life to God, that is it. However, surrender is an ongoing, consistent thing. So often, with my personality type, and probably a lot of other people, I don't like to sit in the discomfort, the desert, or the silence of waiting for Him to speak the next thing. Or those times when He's pulling things to the surface and holding them in front of you, saying, "Hey, these are things I want to deal with inside of you." It's uncomfortable, and no one wants to just sit in that. I have a tendency to want to take hold of things on my own, charge forward, and get really independent. I get to a place where I think I can do things with my own strength. In this season of my life, I've realized that I need to live in a constant state of surrender.

Surrender is not just a one-time thing that you do when you give your life to Christ. To be a Christ-follower means living in a constant state of surrender to Him, His words, His way, the season, the timing, and His leading. It requires an incredible amount of trust. And the moment I put my trust in myself and depend on my own strength is a moment I start to fail or sink before I realize that I'm doing it again. I realize I need to pull back and go back to that place of surrender where I'm relying on His strength, trusting in Him, and waiting on Him. My kind of independent personality is a challenge for me. It can be hard. I'm a little bit too independent for my own good. So I've been really working hard to live in a constant state of surrender and hands open. "Here I am, and you can do with me whatever you want."

Never let ministry come before your family.

In my early days of ministry, I talked to people much older than me who have been in ministry their entire lives while simultaneously raising their families. Many of them have admitted that they were taught and told that the ministry is first and that there's nothing more important than that. They also admit that they regret being taught that because it has caused a lot of pain for their children and their families. Some of their children are not walking with the Lord now because of the pain that was caused by them putting ministry ahead of their family. When I've asked them, "What advice would you give to me as a mother who's raising her children in ministry?" All of the answers have been unanimous. They all say, "Don't ever let ministry come before your family." They learned the hard way. Always keep your family first and above everything else. They are your first ministry. If you can't lead your children to the Lord, how are you going to lead anyone else to the Lord? And if your family isn't healthy, then what are you doing?

I make sure my kids know that they are the most important thing to me, and when they need me, they get me. I've had to cancel things because I had a sick baby. We spend a lot of time on the road, and I can tell when they feel like they're done and want to be home. So immediately that's it—we're done, we go home, and will spend a year at home. Then toward the end of that year—they're actually doing this right now—they're saying, "When are we going back on the bus? When are we going to go to the hotel?" They're ready to get back out.

Now, when I say, "Hey, I'm going to go lead worship," they'll say, "Oh, are you going to go help people find Jesus?" "Yup. That's what I'm going to do." They'll pray for me before I walk out, and that way, they get to be a part of what's happening. When we hear testimonies of what God has done through the music or the worship, we tell them. We share with them, and they get to be a part of that. I recognize that it's not just my sacrifice, but it's also a sacrifice for them. It's important to honor and recognize that we're all in this together. And be sensitive to where they're at and how they're feeling with all of it. I make sure they know that our family comes first.

15

We The Kingdom

We The Kingdom is a multigenerational family of musicians, including producers and songwriters Ed Cash (Chris Tomlin, NeedToBreathe, Bethel Music, Crowder), Scott Cash, Franni Rae Cash, Martin Cash, and Andrew Bergthold. The band organically formed at a Young Life camp in Georgia. Each of the five members came to lead worship, but they themselves were weary and heartbroken due to a number of difficult circumstances. Late one night, as they spontaneously gathered to write a song for the campers, their collaboration caught fire, bringing with it personal healing and a fresh dream for the future.

IG: @wethekingdom

wethekingdom.com

What is worship?

I highly doubt the early church would say, "Hey, we're going to put five people up on stage, and everybody else needs to follow them." It's probably much more like eight of us in a circle, or 800, or 8,000 of us. We really need to be reminded to worship in such a way that we're not exalting any of the people on stage and that it's something we're all doing together. Our heart is for the global church to worship God together.

One really special thing about being a part of We The Kingdom is that we are always bringing other people on stage with us. We did a conference a bit ago, found some worship leaders in the crowd, and got them up on stage to do some songs with them. I looked up, and there were literally 100–150 people on stage with us. It was a really beautiful moment because it reminded me again that worship is not about a person or a band.

What are you worshiping?

Worship is in the DNA of every person. We are going to worship something. There's no way around it. I watched a video recently that actually inspired a song. It was a short video of a Bon Jovi concert singing one of their huge hits. There was not a hand in that audience that wasn't raised reaching out. I was blown away, and I thought, *Wow, what are you reaching for?* There's something in our body and even in our spirit that just wants to natively respond physically.

We want to clap, we want to raise our hands, and we want to scream when we see something awesome.

We've seen it all too often where, whether it's of their own making or not, pastors and worship leaders get elevated beyond the places they should. People start looking at them like, "Ah, you're amazing!" We want and have a tendency to elevate people, and I think it's really dangerous. Our hope is to put the emphasis where it belongs, which is on the Lord.

Stop holding back and bring your mess to God.

Oftentimes, we live under the impression that God only wants us when we're cleaned up on Sunday morning, when we look good and haven't sinned in a week. In reality, God wants us to bring our mess to Him and be honest with Him. He's not afraid of our darkness or brokenness. That's the God of the Bible. He meets us in our craziness, and He's so gracious to us.

The wild thing is, He wants us to bring our mess to Him because you can't really have a true connection with someone unless you show them the mess. A lot of the time, I think we are afraid of being vulnerable with God, and we miss out on having a really deep connection with Him. I love David's relationship with God that we see in the Psalms. God calls him a man after his own heart, but he's sleeping with Bathsheba and murdering her husband. I think the thing about him is that he isn't afraid to bring his mess to God. He isn't afraid for it to be dark. He isn't afraid to question. He asks, "Why have you forsaken me, God? Why have you left me alone? Why have you let my enemies triumph over me? Why have you turned your face from me?" And then he praises God. Sometimes we just look at the praise, and we don't talk about the mess. Even Jesus, saying, "God, why have you turned away from me?" had pain.

Without darkness, there's no light.

I have a hard time dealing with pain. I was reading about Jesus on the cross and thinking about how we often try to hide or avoid our pain. When He was on the cross, the soldiers asked Him if He wanted the vinegar mix, and He turned it down. I was confused at first because I wouldn't want to drink vinegar, but during that time, the concoction they gave him was a painkiller. He turned it away because He wanted to feel the weight of the pain, the heaviness, and the darkness. I love that because we need to be able to face our pain and our darkness. We talk about our pain, and we look at the darkness so that we can see the light. I read this quote the other day that said, "If you numb the dark, then you numb the light." What it was saying is that if you suppress all of your darker emotions, pain, and trauma, then you won't fully experience joy. I think in our relationship with God, the goal is to have a complete connection with Him. But to do that, we have to face our pain and darkness. It's not something to be ashamed of, but it's just all the more incentive to run to the Father and find that healing, find that wholeness that we need.

16

Emmy Rose

Emmy Rose is a worship leader and songwriter at Bethel Church in Redding, CA. Emmy appears on Bethel Music's VICTORY album singing "Promises" and toured with Bethel Music for their 2019 Victory Tour. She also sings "Standing In Miracles" from Bethel Music's HOMECOMING album. Emmy has immersed herself in all aspects of worship within the church, including leading worship for Bethel Church Services and songwriting.

IG: @emmyrose_

Leaders find their confidence in the Lord.

I've noticed that powerful leaders aren't threatened by the greatness in others. To be a powerful leader, you can't be insecure because insecurity doesn't make space for other people's gifts. As worship leaders, we need to build our confidence with the Lord. It's that inner confidence that isn't easily shaken and doesn't easily fall prey to the mindset of competition and comparison.

I've learned a lot about that while being surrounded by so many talented people at Bethel. I've been building my identity and ministry with the Lord and learning to trust Him in every area of my life. It's important to establish yourself in who you are with the Lord so that whatever setting you go into, whether it's in the church or not, you can thrive and have a sustainable long-term ministry that's not built on anything but the Lord. Because those things can fail, but Jesus won't.

Spontaneous and prophetic worship.

Operating in spontaneous worship is a journey for sure. I always want to encourage people to build a history with the Lord first. It's important to be rooted in the word. As simple as that is, I feel like it can't be overstated when it comes to spontaneous worship. If you don't have that history of knowing what the Lord sounds like and how He's chosen to present Himself to us through the word, you don't have those bearings of His character. Without this foundation, it can easily become more emotional or process-oriented rather than something that lines up with who I know the Lord to be and who He's been consistently in His word. Having that foundation of knowing what the Lord sounds like comes from who we've seen Him be through the word. I allow Him to speak to me through scripture and through others in my community.

So, first, build that foundation until you feel confident about your relationship with the Lord and your knowledge of who He is. The next step is learning to hear and discern for yourself. Before you try to give a prophetic word to others, ask yourself, "Can I hear the Lord speaking specifically to me? Has He ever spoken to me?" If so, "What does that sound like? What does it feel like? How can I measure it against who I know Him to be in his word?" We have to test it and hold it to what is good. It's good to step out and practice in safe environments. It's important to recognize the Lord's voice as He's speaking to you before you try to tell other people what the Lord is saying to them.

Practice in your community first.

Community is a great way to flesh out a prophecy. I think sometimes we mystify it, and we're like, "Oh, you either hear them or you don't, and you're either really good at it, or you're not." However, I think there's a lot of steps in-between. So, start by going to a pastor and saying, "Hey,

I just heard this from the Lord in worship. What do you think about that?" If you're in a community that's safe and they want to explore that too, then you can get feedback and learn to hear the Lord's voice. You can filter it through people and ask what they think.

Then if you're released in leadership to go for it, go for it! You can practice singing out what you feel the Lord wants to do in the room. It can be super simple at first. It's important not to add to what you hear. I love that Jesus says He only ever said what He heard the Father say, and He only did what He saw the Father do. So it could be as simple as "he loves you" or "he's meeting you today." Maybe that's all you heard, so you sing that. And then, for the one person who really didn't want to be there or really wasn't sure about coming, hearing that simple foundational truth may be exactly what they needed to hear.

Practicing this is so important. Practice by yourself. Practice in community. Practice in smaller settings so that you're prepared to do it with the congregation. This is the best way that I've found to do it. I never want to feel like I'm venturing past something that I'm not released to do. But if you're released to do it by the leadership at your church, practice, practice, practice. Like anything else, it's a muscle, and we have to exercise it.

Practical tips for prophesying *outside* of the church.

I've had moments when I was outside the church at a coffee shop or mall or something, and the Lord had spoken to me about someone. Those moments feel a little bit riskier because sometimes it's someone whom I don't even know. I like to phrase it like, "Hey, sometimes I hear from God. Would it be okay if I shared something with you that I felt like He was saying?" I usually try to make it as diffused as possible for them and me because I want it to be a conversation, and I want it to lead them to the Lord.

Another way that you could start off is by saying, "Hey, I feel like I hear from God sometimes, and I'm trying to practice saying it when I feel something for someone. Would it be okay if I shared that with you?" I try to make it to where it doesn't put pressure on them or on me. Most people are probably pretty curious to hear what God has to say about them, so most people are pretty open.

Practical tips for prophesying *inside* of the church.

If I'm prophesying to someone in church, I might say something like, "Hey, I feel like God gave me a word for you. Can I share it with you?" I will often ask them if it's okay if I put my hand on them, and I'll kind of pray/speak it. That way, they're not looking at me the whole time. I like to softly and gently give it to them as a gift.

Afterward, I'll usually ask, "Hey, does that resonate with

you? Does that make sense?" You can also say, "Feel free to take that to the Lord and see what He says about it."

You might not get it right all the time.

When you prophetically speak over a room or even one person, it might not resonate with 100% of them. But that doesn't mean that it's not accurate. It might be the timing. It could be something for them years down the road. Even if you get it wrong, if your heart is pure and you're doing it out of compassion and out of love, it's going to do a work in someone's life simply because your foundation is the Word of God. And the Word of God accomplishes its purposes. It won't return void.

It's like sowing seed. Whatever happens with that seed is really not up to you. Sometimes we try to overly control it, or we try to put it in a prettier package, add to it, or maybe even take away from it because prophesying can be uncomfortable. But in those moments, the Lord reminds me that the only thing I'm accountable for is to hear His voice and do.

When receiving a prophetic word, it's good to receive the meat and spit out the bones. Take what's good from it, and don't hold onto the things that don't line up with the Word of God.

What not to do when prophesying.

Sometimes we put so much pressure on ourselves that we forget our humanity and forget to be humble. This can cause us to overcompensate and make it uncomfortable for the other person. The moment that I say, "I can't be wrong," I might as well give up in the kingdom. Because anything in ministry takes risk. We aren't in it to be perfect; we're in it to be obedient. Even if your prophetic word is wrong, have a humble heart and say, "If that doesn't resonate, feel free to let it go." Even if that's the case, I know that I fulfilled my job because I was obedient. It's mysterious how God moves and how God speaks.

The purpose of prophecy.

Prophecy is to build people up. It's to edify them, not to tear them down. But if you ever feel like it's being used in the wrong way, you have every right to be like, "Hey, I don't feel like that is actually edifying, or I don't feel like that's something that I want to receive." Prophecy is a gift to be used by the Lord and is not something you're qualified to do on your own or entitled to. Don't lose your spirit of humility and your spirit of dependency on the Lord.

17

Gable Price

Gable Price is known as the frontman for the band Gable Price and Friends. Referred to consistently as "The Killers if they were a Christian band," Gable Price and Friends treads the fine line between Christian music and just plain rock & roll. Gable is also a worship leader and songwriter featured on Bethel Music's recent album HOMECOMING.

IG: @gablepat

gablepriceandfriends.com

Getting turned down at Bethel to writing and recording on a Bethel album.

When I moved out to Redding, I auditioned for the worship team at Bethel School of Ministry, and I didn't get in. I tried out to be a worship leader every year of school, and I never got it. After three years of trying and not getting accepted, I was really discouraged because I felt like everything had been leading up to me doing this. I wondered what I would do because I had always wanted to be a worship leader but felt like I could never be one because I wasn't making the cut. This is a story about not giving up on your calling because fast-forward years later, and I got to write and sing the title track for Bethel's *HOMECOMING* record with Cory Asbury.

If God's calling you to do something, do it.

I grew up in an environment where everyone is amazingly talented. That has been the hardest thing for me because I've always grown up with people older than me, bigger than me, and more talented than me. Being content has been really hard, and in some ways, that's good. If I could have seen where I'm at now, I don't know if I would have been able to believe it. I've gotten to meet so many incredible people and have been able to do so many amazing things. But even in all of that, there are still times when I still struggle with anxiety.

Spiritual amnesia is the best way to put it. It's so easy to forget about what God has done in your life. We have to stand firm on his faithfulness and continually remind ourselves of how he's been with us throughout our entire journey.

When I think back to when I was in my first year at Bethel School of Ministry, and I didn't get to do anything musical, it was really just the start for me. I had gotten turned down to be a worship leader and as a guitarist. I thought, *If I could just lead worship, the Lord and I would be in this great place. If I could just have a place to lead worship, I would have a really special time with God.* But my problem wasn't not getting to lead worship at Bethel; my problem was with how I viewed the situation. If you have God calling you to do something, find ways to do it and make the best of your current season.

I have a ton of people that reach out to me, and they say if they could just move out to Bethel and worship God there, then things would be amazing. I try to encourage them to run with it where they live. God is the same where they live as he is here at Bethel. The grass is always greener on the other side. This is true in so many areas of our lives, including our spiritual life.

18

Dante Bowe

Dante Bowe joined Bethel Music as a worship leader and songwriter in June 2019 and can be seen leading worship on their tours and at Bethel Church. Dante lives in Columbus, Georgia, where he is a Worship Pastor at Addereth Church and a songwriter with Maverick City Music.

IG: @dantebowe

dantebowe.com

Falling in love with Jesus.

At 16 years old, I had an encounter with God in my room that changed everything. I was worshiping while listening to a Kierra Sheard album, and I got saved and filled with the Holy Spirit on my bedroom floor. That was my moment of transformation. Later on in life, I discovered the love of God. It wasn't just about religion; it started becoming more of a friendship. It was about being and understanding. I started loving to grow and loving to be stretched. It shifted from trying not to go to Hell to having a friendship and relationship with a loving Jesus.

Leading worship.

I feel clearer and more focused when I lead worship these days because I have a better understanding of my need to be dependent on God and of the Lordship that Jesus holds. Starting off worship with recognizing that out loud, saying the name of Jesus, and lifting His name high changes everything in the room.

Even in our writing camps at Maverick City, we really focus on the Lordship of God. When you hear the song "You Keep On Getting Better" or "Promises," it's a declaration of God's lordship. "I put my trust in Jesus, my anchor to the ground, my hope and firm foundation…" We're declaring who He is. He's strong. He's not weak. That's who He is.

Being stretched to grow.

One of my spiritual leaders, Eddie James, told me the best way to make people hungry is to eat in front of them. If you've ever been hungry and you see someone eating something, it makes you crave that thing they're eating. So, as worship leaders, we have to work toward freedom in ourselves. When people see that freedom evident in you, naturally, you're going to begin to change the culture because people will hunger for that freedom you're exuding. People will start saying, "What is that? I want to sing to Jesus like that." It doesn't even have to be dancing or singing, it could just be in the way you talk or in the way you live your life.

As worshipers and worship leaders, if we truly become free, naturally, the people we lead will have to align with that or be uncomfortable. It's one or the other. And it's okay if people are uncomfortable; that can be a gateway to freedom. Most things that the Lord is going to stretch us on will be really uncomfortable. As we become free, they become free, and as we eat and feast, they want to eat and feast. Hungry people awaken hunger in other people.

19

Hillsong UNITED
Benjamin Hastings
& Dylan Thomas

Birthed in the youth ministry of Hillsong Church in 1998, UNITED is arguably one of the most influential worship bands of all time. Hillsong UNITED has released 16 albums and with that received 16 Dove Awards and numerous Billboard chart-topping songs like "Oceans (Where Feet May Fail)," "So Will I (100 Billion X)," "Whole Heart (Hold Me Now)," "Touch The Sky," "Hosanna," "Lead Me To The Cross," and many more.

IG: @benjaminwilliamhastings

IG: @dylanthomas

IG: @hillsongUNITED

hillsong.com/united

Ben's first memory of Hillsong UNITED.

I grew up in Ireland and became a Christian when I was 15 years old. I remember one time I was on holiday with my family and I went into an old CD store. I randomly saw the cover of the UNITED album "Look To You" and thought it looked cool. Having no idea what it was, I just bought it. That was like my first experience of Hillsong UNITED. The songs really shaped me and made me fall in love with worship music. I was already writing songs, but this record definitely steered me toward writing songs about God. Fast-forward ten years, and I'm friends with all the guys and get to be a part of the team.

Dylan's first memory of Hillsong UNITED.

As a teenager, I was actually in the crowd when we recorded "Look To You" and some of the other UNITED albums. These were anchoring moments in my life because I was already playing music. My dad was a songwriter and a musician, so I grew up around music. It was amazing to think that I could attach music to a purpose that is so much greater than just being a rock star or anything like that.

I got connected to Joel and Marty Sampson because my dad managed their mainstream band. I grew up around mainstream music and saw a lot of the rockstar world as well, but it was so cool to see people with an amazing relationship with God creating music that had such a greater purpose than just singing about broken hearts. I remember being at some of those early recordings and just saying, "Oh, this is what I want to do." I didn't know at the time that I wanted to do it with UNITED or be a part of UNITED. I just knew that I wanted to sew into a local church, so I started playing in the kids' ministry and eventually in the youth ministry.

Dylan – The music we create is more than just songs.

It's been an amazing journey being anchored in music that really is so much more than just writing songs for the sake of writing songs, but creating melodies that draw people closer to God. We truly hold it with such reverence that God would even continue to use us to be a part of people's journeys. Recently, in our church staff meeting, they shared this testimony of a guy who grew up a Christian and later walked away from God, but he still listened to the music. He told the pastor that he ended up coming back to church and God because of the music. It was such a sobering moment to know that God used us to play a part in that story to some degree. So, thinking back to being in the crowd and then being part of the team and experiencing a moment like that, it was so humbling and something I'll never take for granted.

Running rehearsals.

We are really intentional with our rehearsals. We rehearse so that we're able to create a space of spontaneity. We'll have the setlist so structured and the songs so dialed in that we can create space and leave room for the Holy Spirit to move. Spontaneity comes from a place of preparation.

Because we've played the songs so many times as a band, we'll spend the majority of our rehearsals running through transitions. We'll have the band play the last 16 bars and run the transition because that's one of the most important parts. You spend so much time working on the songs that you want to make sure you don't mess it up during the transition. Because transitions are the most optimal time for there to be a distraction. Sometimes silence between songs can be very helpful (especially if silence is used as an instrument), but most of the time, we'll make the songs flow together seamlessly.

We place high importance on stewarding our gifts. We want to bring our absolute best because for us, if we can bring our best and represent Jesus as best as we possibly can, then He can just come in and do what only He can do.

Preparing setlists.

Creating setlists is all about the journey. You have to think about where you want to get to, how long you have to get there, and what materials you are working with. Ask yourself what songs you know you'll use, and then what other songs will help take people on a journey. Creating a great setlist has to do a lot with timing, dynamics, patience, and what keys the songs are in. Understand and learn the circle of fifths. It will really help if you utilize that. And again, the more you prepare, the more you can operate in spontaneous moments and setlist changes.

Utilizing a talk-back mic.

I have a microphone that talks to the band and vocalists when I'm on stage. When I'm on the talk-back mic, I'm watching the worship leaders the whole time. I'm really trusting and following the worship leaders and being attentive to where they want to go next. If I'm sensing something, or if I can see that something's happening off script, I actually just say, "Hey, heads up, guys."

Oftentimes, musicians are playing and looking down, so saying "heads up" really grabs everyone's attention. It brings us back as a collective worship team and causes people to pay attention as we're going somewhere. Worship leaders know that they can give me a cue or turn around and give direction at any time, and I'll communicate that with the band. This helps us all be on the same page and flow smoothly.

It's so important for the worship leader and the music director to have a great relationship and clear communication. The music director needs to remember always to stay calm and collected when they are communicating with the band, even if things are going wrong.

20

Aaron Moses

—

Aaron Moses is a worship leader and songwriter whose songs reveal so much about his heart and fire for the Lord. He's written songs like "Promises," "Be Praised," "Yahweh," and so many more. He's a part of the Maverick City community and someone who has impacted so many other communities over the years.

IG: @aaronmosesofficial

Worship leaders, what is your identity?

One of the things that the enemy targets now more than ever in our generation is identity. The enemy's greatest fear is for you to step into the fullness of who God created you to be. A lot of worship leaders hang their identity on what they do. I've heard it said that we were never created to be human "doings," but to be human "beings." We're created to become like Him. One thing that God taught me is that He never created us unto our gift. He created our gift unto us. The gift He gave us was for us to use for His glory. If it were the other way around, He would have created the gift first.

He deposited a treasure inside of everybody that would be given unto them to use for His glory. Worship leaders, the gift of singing was never given to us to make it our foundation and what we identify with. He gave that to us to give back to Him for his glory. Scripturally, before Jesus ever performed a miracle, the Bible says that the Father was pleased with him. When he got baptized, and the dove came down, and the heavens opened up, God said, "This is my son in whom I am well pleased."

A mentor of mine told me that we do everything "from" and not "for" Affirmation. We're already affirmed. We already identify as sons and daughters. And when He looks at us, He doesn't see singers, worship leaders, or songwriters. He sees a son who can lead, who can write, who can produce, or whatever your gifting is. The worst thing to do is to hang all you are on what you do. Because God forbid one day that's stripped away, what are you going to do? Who are you? For me, these last few years, that's been my journey. Who am I if you take the singing, songwriting, or producing away? God has been teaching me that. And if there's anything I can encourage worship leaders, songwriters, and artists to do, it's to take time to learn who you are. Strip all that stuff away because one day, you're going to stand alone. And the last thing you want to do is to make your foundation what you do. Because that was never the intention of Jesus.

The reason you can sing is not so that you can be on a stage in front of a hundred thousand people. The reason you can sing is so that when you go in the presence of Jesus, you can sing to Him. You can sing to Him, and He can sing over you. You can call Him a beautiful savior, and He can call you a beautiful son. You can call Him master, and He can call you son and friend. And that's just the point of our giftings. To lead us back to Him. He put treasures in jars of clay so that every treasure could lead back to him.

Comparing yourself to everyone else.

A lot of my lack of identity was because I was comparing myself to everybody else and what God was doing with them. God had to sit me down and teach me to be okay with where I was. And if there's anybody that's dealing with constantly comparing yourself to everybody around you, know that where you are and where He has you right now is on purpose. It's not a coincidence where He has you, and it's not by mistake. If you want to kill the spirit of comparison, celebrate someone else. For two years, He was teaching me to be okay with where I was and who I was because I was fearfully and wonderfully made.

It doesn't come from the platforms. And that's what I was seeking, the platforms, the next opportunity, and God just stripped that away. Not because I was unable to do what He gave me to do on those platforms, but because He knew that if He had let me go without knowing who I was, these platforms would have destroyed me. And now I've found my identity in God. I'm so confident in who I am, knowing that what He made was perfect. And I've heard it said that when you have a lack of identity, or when you're not confident in what God has placed in you, that's actually an insult to what He made. He said you're fearfully and wonderfully made. So. when you think otherwise, that's an insult to what He said was good. From the beginning, He created you in His sight, and He said it was good.

21

Pat Barrett

Pat Barrett is best known as one of the primary singers/songwriters for the band Housefires. He's someone that is filled with passion, energy, and someone Chris Tomlin says is the craziest person he's ever been on tour with. With songs such as "Build My Life" and "Good Good Father," Pat is impacting worship communities across the globe in a massive way.

IG: @patbarrett

Patbarrettmusic.com

The door blew off the RV—I should have listened.

When I was 20 years old, getting ready to go on a worship tour, every single person we had ever met, every mentor, every voice of reason told us, "Whatever you do, do not buy an old RV and try to turn it into a bus." They said, "Just get a van and deal with it." So guess what, we got the RV against all better judgment. I remember driving up to Tulsa in this old RV we'd just bought, going 70 mph down the highway, and we started to hear this light shaking sound. Then all of a sudden, the main door of the RV blew off while we were going down the highway. The person sitting at the dinette in the living area saw the door fly off and over the cars that were behind us.

The best part is that we were already late, so we didn't even stop. We were still going down the highway with 70 mph winds blowing through the entire RV. At that point, we had to admit that we should have listened. Most of my life is like that in retrospect. I really should have listened to… well… everybody.

Authenticity frees other people.

When I meet someone who is comfortable in their own skin, it frees me to be comfortable in mine. I think that's why I value when I'm around people that are so okay with being themselves. For whatever reason, it unlocks the opportunity for other people to do that too. In fact, I've also found the opposite to be true. When you're around someone, and you feel like you're not talking to the person, you're talking to the persona, that actually encourages hiding and pretending. I know that sometimes the scariest thing is to be yourself. But if you can get to the point where you don't have to present yourself in a way that you're not, then you find acceptance from people and know that they really like you and not just this version of you. They don't like worship leader Pat or ministry Pat; they just like Pat. That is what real friendships and relationships are like. When people like the pretend version of you, that's one of the loneliest feelings you can have. It's all about relationships and being connected to one another, yourself, and God. Jesus doesn't deal with the pretend you.

Worship leaders are being used.

I remember a friend of mine, Jason Upton, was talking about the desire that we have to be used by God. We always ask God to use us. And I remember him asking the question, have you ever liked being used in any other setting? Is that term a positive thing? I can't remember ever being excited that a person used me. Wouldn't you rather be loved than be used? Isn't there something more than just your utility that makes you precious to God? I know how difficult it can be at times as a worship leader, or someone in leadership, to just be loved by God instead of used by Him where we find our purpose in our utility instead of our purpose in being with God.

Gratitude is not reactionary.

Encourage yourself to live today like it's a gift and not a burden. That type of joy and gratitude is an inside job. It's not a symptom of something else. I don't have joy because something else gave me joy. Like, of course, that can be true, but the inner work of gratitude is not reactionary. You CAN just decide to be grateful. And once you make that decision, then all of a sudden, you'll find yourself being thankful for a lot of things that you would never have thought. And now, nothing can steal that gratitude and happiness from you.

Being fearful vs. being in the moment.

My grandmother passed away a few days ago while she was in hospice care at my parents' house. And she was one of those people that loved the Lord. She always had the women's intercessory Wednesday prayer group. She had a life well-lived. When my parents called me and told me she had passed away, I had a memory of a phone call that I got from her a couple of years ago, right before I put out my first studio solo album. This was a point in my life where I was terrified. I was scared of the future. I felt a new chapter starting in my life and all other chapters coming to a close, and I felt insecure. I felt like I was trusting in the dark and doing my best to follow the voice of God, but also having that feeling of hoping that I was hearing Him right.

So, she called me and gave me this word about not

being fearful of the future. It was something that was really important to me. I was stuck in the future, terrified of it, and missing the moment I was in. Then she passed away. And when I heard the news, I had a memory of that word. Because you know what, I'm in that same boat again. I've got so many question, and everyone's wondering what's going on in the world, and what if, what if, what if. I have that feeling in my heart knowing that the Lord spoke to me from her before, and I listened. Now I'm going to listen again. And that's what life feels like right now for me. You're caught up in tomorrow, and you can get fearful, but we've been given enough for today. Sometimes that's a song, sometimes that's being quiet and listening, sometimes that's finding communion with friends. But all the time, it's gratefulness, gratitude, and being thankful for today. For any songwriters and worship leaders, I encourage you to continually write from that place of where it matters today. What we sing matters today. The way we lead matters today. And it matters in this moment right now. The more I focus on today, the less fearful I am of tomorrow. And the more excited I get about right now.

22

Matt Redman

Matt Redman is a worship leader, songwriter, and true legend from Watford, England. He's played venues like Madison Square Garden, Wembley Stadium, and the Royal Albert Hall and recorded in iconic studios, such as Abbey Road in London and Capitol Records in LA. Matt's best-known songs include "The Heart of Worship," "Blessed Be Your Name," "Our God," and the double-Grammy-winning "10,000 Reasons." His more recent songs include "Do It Again" and "Build my Life."

IG: @mattredmanmusic

mattredman.com

Losing his dad to suicide. Abuse. And how worship heals.

I started playing guitar when I was a teenager simply because I wanted to play the worship songs I was hearing at church. I had a real turbulent childhood. I lost my dad to suicide when I was seven years old, and after that, I dealt with some abusive situations. It was a really tough time. But one of the things that kept me stable and sane was worship music. It's funny because people always ask me, "How did you start writing songs?" Well, the reason is, really, because I needed to write songs. And I needed a way to pour out my heart to God. I needed to sing some truth. I found it a natural way of talking to God and such a reassuring thing to do. So, I got into it really early on.

Know your strengths and surround yourself with people who complement your gifts.

I didn't come from a musical background or musical training. Lyrics will probably always be my strongest thing. I've tried to do the best I can to surround myself with people who know what they're doing when it comes to music.

The origins of "Heart of Worship."

It's funny because the lyrics of "Heart of Worship" are a literal description of what happened in our church. Our pastor felt that we'd gone off track a little bit with our worship, and we were making it into this consuming activity of "I like this song. I don't like that song. I like this worship leader. I don't like that one. It's too loud. It's too quiet." And he said what we should be thinking about was what we were bringing as an offering to God. So, he said for the next few weeks, we were going to turn off the sound system and the band, and we were just going to get in a room with our Bibles, our hearts, and our voices and just check that we could still find our way to a place of worship. And that was an uncomfortable time. I was wondering, *Well, what am I going to do? Am I fired?*

It was a weird time, but then it actually turned into a really beautiful moment as we realized that we could still do this. We could throw ourselves into this. We could draw near to God, He could draw near to us, we could lift our voices together and see the truth. So when I wrote the song, I was just describing what happened. *When the music fades, all is stripped away. And I simply come. Longing just to bring something that's of worth, that will bless your heart. I'll bring you more than a song.* And then, of course, the chorus on coming back to the heart of worship.

Choosing what you're going to write a song about.

I think you obviously take your biggest cues from scripture, but you also have to take them from your community, life, and what your church family is walking through. Or what is happening right now in society and the news, and writing into this moment. There's so much instability around us, so much uncertainty, so many unknowns. So, it's a really good time to sing truth and sing about stability, competency, and how steadfast the name of Jesus is. You've always got to have your antenna up as a songwriter. I'm tuning it up to what's going on in the world, what's going on in our church family, or what the pastor is preaching. Those are the kind of things that make such a difference.

23

Kari Jobe

Kari Jobe is someone that I've watched model a pure pursuit before the Lord for so long. She's arguably one of the most influential worship leaders and Christian artists on the planet, but you'd never know that about her by her countenance and the way that she loves people. She has two Grammy nominations as well as written and recorded anthems like "Forever," "Revelation Song," and "The Blessing."

IG: @karijobe

karijobe.com

Bringing a deeper culture of worship to your church.

When I was young, there was a season for me when I was serving at my church, but I wasn't getting to use my gift to lead. I was serving and singing on the team but not really getting to lead worship. I felt God was calling my community and me to a deeper level of worship. So, I asked my parents if I could do some nights of worship at our house and invited some friends of mine that I knew really loved worship. I also had a friend that played guitar, so I asked if he would come play on Friday nights. And soon, we had this little worship band called Throne Room Worship.

It was after around 65 people showed up in our living room one Friday that my parents finally decided it was time to move it out of the house. So then we asked churches in the area if we could use their buildings on Friday nights, and everybody was always so open to it. It was such a cool experience. Through this, I felt like the Lord honored me for wanting to have a place where I could use and grow my gift of prophetic and spontaneous worship. In a lot of church cultures, there's not a lot of time to do any flowing. Which is fine because there are so many people that churches need to facilitate for a weekend service. However, if God has called you to this, there is still always a way.

So, if I could sum this up, I'd say don't be limited by the culture. You can change a culture. It does take time, and it's not something that can be done by being pushy or manipulative. The Lord will not honor that, but He will honor your heart to want to facilitate a move of the presence of God. Ask your church, the worship team, or some people if they want to get together on a Friday night at someone's house. So you can just worship and get to know each other on a deeper level. And don't be limited by what you think your culture is. You may be inspired to help change it.

If your heart is burning to do something new or to see the worship in your church go to a new level, ask God to speak to you and show you what He wants you to do with that. Then just obey what you hear.

The dark night of the soul.

For anyone feeling like God is far away or you're not hearing Him speak, know that these times are also what makes a relationship go to a deeper place. You're in a dark night of the soul, and you have two choices. You can either go left or go right. You could go to a place of not wanting to do the hard work of your heart and going after the Lord, or you could go after the Lord and hold on for dear life. You can ask the Lord, "What do you want to show me through this? Because I'm not leaving." That's when your relationship is taken to the next level.

You don't know God as a healer unless you need him to heal. And you don't need Him to be a comforter unless you need to be comforted. Not that we want to go through those hard things because we don't, but I do appreciate those seasons when He knew I could handle it.

The beauty in being vulnerable.

I don't know any leaders in my life that have done anything without being broken, real, and honest. And the ones that I've seen in my 20 years of doing ministry that weren't open and vulnerable, there was a lot going on under the surface, and they ended up not doing ministry anymore. Being authentic and letting people know that we're all in this together is a beautiful part of leadership. It's okay to say, "Hey, I'm in the midst of something really difficult, but this is what God's been saying." That simple act will always help someone.

I've led worship in those places before, and I've had just to stop and say, "I'm really in the midst of something and God's working on my heart. And I feel extremely emotional today. So I just need you to sing this out and actually need you to sing this over me." I've done that. And those were times when it felt really powerful. I was in that place when my sister lost her baby. I remember having to lead worship on that Friday right after the funeral, and I didn't want to. I had every right to cancel. But my pastor at the time met with me and really helped me. She said she thought I should go on Friday and just be myself because there are so many women that are in the midst of intense pain and heartache. I should go and share what God's doing because it will be impactful. And it was.

People don't care what you sound like.

When getting to lead worship on a scale of where God has taken me, there is a stewarding of the call and the influence that is so precious to me. I will always cherish and honor that I get to do this. But there's also aching for going back to the sacred. I'm realizing now that people have always wanted that. They want the sacred, raw, and authentic presence of God. They don't want fluff. They don't care about the lights. They don't care about what it sounds like. If it has encounter locked up in it, that's what people are connecting with. That's what we're all in pursuit of. And as a worship leader, I encourage you to be in that pursuit as well.

24

Naomi Raine

Naomi Raine is a part of the Maverick City collective and has written songs like "The Story I'll Tell," "Pour Me Out," "Getting Ready," and so many others. As you'll read, she is truly someone that is caught up in the beauty of the Lord and passionate about experiencing Him through worship.

IG: @naomiraine

naomirainemusic.com

Vocal cord surgery and trusting God in the transition.

About three years ago, I was in a space mentally where I knew I needed a transition. And at the same time, I was having vocal difficulty and a lot of fatigue in my voice. I had no idea what was going on. I went to the doctor and found out that I had vocal cord polyps. If you're not familiar, those are different from nodules. Nodules go away; polyps don't. They told me that the only way I was going to get rid of them was through surgery. However, there is a 1% chance you can get rid of them with therapy. When you're in a position like that, you try everything. So, I tried the therapy, and it didn't work. Now the doctors were sure I needed to schedule the surgery.

A little fact about me, I can't even get blood drawn, so I'm very concerned about any type of knife near my vocal cords. So I kept putting off the surgery even though I knew that I would eventually have to do it in the back of my mind. My voice is my gift and what I believe the Lord is using in my life. I made the decision to get the surgery, and shortly after, I had this huge opportunity to go to Nashville that I knew I needed to take. I felt like this was something that God was doing. However, the surgery was scheduled on the same day I was supposed to be in Nashville.

So, by faith, I decided not to get the surgery, and I was super afraid to tell my doctor. I would not suggest anyone do that, but I didn't go. I ended up going to Nashville, and it was at that moment that I had sung "Pour Me Out" in a room that just so happened to have Todd Delaney and the president of E1 gospel. God used that moment to kickstart this whole thing for me. When I went back and got my vocal cords checked, the polyps were gone. It was only by faith. God gave me two options. "Are you going to believe me, or are you going to trust in your talent and try to do it on your own strength?" That was a big lesson for me. As a side note, I do not endorse nor would I ever tell someone not to get the surgery they need. But I believe, for me, this was the lesson and experience I had to have. I definitely need my voice, but if I'm not reliant on his spirit, then all of this is for nothing.

The questions worship leaders should be asking.

There are some videos that came out of me leading worship, and I'm looking crazy. I didn't have time to change before we filmed and I was looking like a mess. With Maverick City, we've always had a just-come-as-you-are attitude. However, once a video starts to hit a million views, you start to think to yourself, *Maybe I should brush my hair more.* Or, *Maybe I should put on a little mascara because I'm looking a little crazy.* And when the videos started coming out, I quickly had to die to that. It really doesn't matter. I told myself, "Naomi, you gotta die." That has to be my default. I have to tell you that this has been the hardest work of my life not to be thinking about myself, how I sound, what I look like, or what I'm doing. I know that all of that stuff just doesn't matter.

The questions we should be asking are: Did we worship

God? Did we give Him everything? Did we give Him something? Because if we did, He's pleased with that. I'm convinced that we're too hard on ourselves when it comes to worship. We know that there are things that are acceptable and not acceptable, but because Jesus came and was that perfect sacrifice, I know that I don't have to do this perfectly for it to be acceptable. I'm already accepted. He's already good with me. He loves me, and if I mess up, okay. We'll get it next time. I just can't live in that space anymore. It's exhausting. And when you do, you end up coming home and being a jerk to people that love you and want to spend time with you.

I want to worship God. It doesn't need to be the next big hit. I just want to worship Him. I just want to give Him what's real for me, my heart, my love, and whatever I have.

Speaking to all leaders.

My concern is that in this generation, because we're a YouTube generation, that sometimes the congregation and the members are actually getting more than the leaders are. Because we, as leaders, we're still in performance mode while the people are getting, giving, or on the floor experiencing God. Yet, the leaders and the ministers are the ones that are still trying to perform and to be this certain persona. And we could be missing it the whole time. I challenge you to step out of the persona and just be your real authentic self.

25

Chris Tomlin

Chris Tomlin is someone who needs no introduction. If you're reading this, you've most likely sung at least one, but probably more, of his songs. He's sold millions of albums, streamed billions of tracks, spawned 16 #1 radio singles, and a list of Grammy, Dove, Billboard Music and American Music Awards. Touted by TIME Magazine as "the most often sung artist anywhere," on any given Sunday, tens of millions of people in churches across the globe sing songs that Chris has written. His benchmark anthems include "Amazing Grace (My Chains Are Gone)," "At the Cross (Love Ran Red)," "Our God," "How Great is our God," and "Good, Good Father."

IG: @christomlin

christomlin.com

Chris on the craziest person he's ever toured with.

That's an easy one. Pat Barrett. He has so much energy it's crazy. Every single time when he walks on stage, he just starts screaming and getting the crowd going. He's just a completely crazy man. Every night, we would go up at the end of the concert and do "God's Great Dance Floor." It was so much fun. And every night, at some point, he'd find somebody who's brought a flag and just start running around on stage with it. There was one night where he was running around, and he grabbed somebody's phone out of the audience. He was running around taking selfies during "God's Great Dance Floor." Then at the end of the song, he walked over to me, leaned in, and said, "I don't remember whose phone this is." So, we had to get on the mic and announce, "If you're missing your phone, please get it after the show."

Best advice for worship leaders.

Worship leaders are my tribe. They're not just people that are like-minded, but people that I love to be around, encourage, listen to, and learn from. We're all in this together, leading the church. Something I'd want to encourage worship leaders with is interestingly something from a song on my newest record called "Be The Moon." It's an interesting idea that I've carried and talked about for a while. When you think about the moon and what it does, it shines light in dark places. However, the moon has no light on its own. It's just reflecting the light from the sun.

I think as a worship leader, when you're on stage and in front of people, there could be pressure to make something happen or do something. However, the moon doesn't strive to do anything. It just is who it is. It just reflects and doesn't have to strive. As a worship leader, that's simply what you do. We just reflect a light that's not coming from us. And this alleviates all of the pressure we put on ourselves. Jesus said you're the light of the world, and that's because we're reflecting His light. Maybe the moon is full and bright some days. And maybe on others, you're just a sliver of light because it's cloudy. This life is hard. The world is tough. It's unfair. And some days, maybe it just feels really cloudy, and that's okay because life is hard. But always know His light is coming, and you're a reflection of that.

That's all you gotta do. There's a line in the song that says, "Everybody wants to be somebody. I want to be somebody too, but if I'm going to be known for something, I want to be known for you. I want to be the moon." The idea is that if you're shining on me, I'm shining right back for you. Getting in that place of being a reflection of God is really what it's all about. And the essence of Christianity and faith.

26

Aodhan King

Aodhan King is a worship leader and songwriter at Hillsong Church in Sydney, Australia. He has been a key part of the Hillsong Young & Free team since the beginning, writing several songs that have become anthems for churches and individuals across the world, such as "Sinking Deep," "Highs And Lows," "Alive," "Brighter," "Back To Life," "In Sync," and many more.

IG: @aodhanking

hillsong.com/youngandfree/

Finding your value outside of your influence.

Staying grounded in God and who I am outside of being "Aodhan from Y&F" is a daily practice. I know a lot of worship leaders can fall into the trap of finding their identity in other things outside of God that really aren't going to fulfill us. When I'm in the thick of it and traveling a lot, it's very easy to forget that my life is not just this. It's not just traveling, writing songs, leading worship, or whatever else goes with that. I learned pretty early on that my value wasn't what I was bringing because if it was, unfortunately, I know I'm not the greatest guitar player, the best songwriter, the greatest singer, and I'm definitely not the best piano player.

That makes you look elsewhere for where your value comes from. Not to be cliché, but for me, I always felt like my value obviously was in God, but it was also in a community of people. And that community is so important to me. My community is my friends, church, and the people around me. I think the temptation is often to put on a show and be this person that you're really not because people have expectations of what a worship leader is supposed to look like. They expect them to be this way or that way, but your best friends know who you really are. And so the moment you start pandering to these expectations that are really not who you are, your friends are gonna reality-check you.

So, realizing that is when I understood what was most important in my life: God, my family, and my closest friends.

Not to say that there isn't a responsibility to being a worship leader. There obviously are moral expectations and the things that I write songs about need to be true. That's really important. All that to say, continuing to find my identity in Christ and not the music is something most worship leaders have to strive for daily. We need good friends and pastors that help keep our focus.

The importance of community.

Every Friday night, our youth ministry runs, and we're in it and around it. I think the reason why that is so important is that Young & Free is the expression of Hillsong's youth ministry, and you need to be around that to know what's going on. Who are the kids? What are the things that kids are dealing with? What's important to them? What do you feel like God wants to say to this group of people, this generation, at this time? And to not be around that wouldn't make any sense. Our community is everything to us.

The controversy of Y&F's music and not being allowed to play it in church.

When we started Young & Free, it was very controversial. We weren't even allowed to sing the songs in church initially. It was an insane time. Our songs were a shock to the system. People in our church were saying that they didn't think we should be singing our songs live because they were too dancey, or it felt like a nightclub. Then Pastor Brian, our senior pastor, stood up and said, "No, we're doing it." The whole thing was definitely a risk, and it was hard in the beginning.

With our newest record, we've steered our sound in a new direction again. Which just feels very natural to us. I think part of why people connect with our music is that we're willing to listen to our community and feel what they're connecting with. At the beginning, people didn't want rock like Hillsong UNITED in 2012; they wanted more EDM. And now people are going away from EDM and wanting more trap and grunge. A lot of our new sound is created by new people in the community, and we just let them be themselves and create the sounds that are true to them.

We can try to do this all on our own, but we need to be anchored in a community of people that calls us higher because community is what pushes us into who we want to become. And that applies in every area of our lives as well.

27

Brian Johnson

Brian Johnson is a titan when it comes to leading people into God's presence. He's a pastor, worship leader, author, and one of the creators of Bethel Music, where he's been an integral part of the production of over 16 albums from Bethel that have influenced the culture of worship across the world. He's written many chart-topping songs that are sung by millions of people every single week like "Goodness of God," "Lion and the Lamb," "Battle Belongs," "Living Hope," "No Longer Slaves," and "One Thing Remains."

IG: @brianjohnsonm

brianandjennjohnson.com

Brian's first worship song ever.

I'm as PK (pastor's kid) as they come. I'm a sixth-generation PK. In fact, when I first took over the worship team at 21, all of my relatives were on the team, including my two grandpas. My dad, now the head pastor of Bethel Church, was also a worship leader who actually taught on worship long before he taught on anything else. I grew up learning about the power of praise and worship. When I was 17 years old, I picked up my brother's guitar for the first time. It was a twelve-string, but he took six strings off to make it a six-string. That's when I became hooked and started playing back-up guitar at our youth group, which led to me writing my first song within two months of learning guitar.

I showed that song to my youth pastor, and he wanted me to lead it at youth. It was a reggae song. Believe it or not, I had dreadlocks back then. And afterward, this lady came up to me and gave me a word about my future in leading worship. That was when I decided that this was what I wanted to do, so I dove full in, and the rest is history.

The origins of Bethel Music and being scrappy.

I remember we had the idea to start this music label because we had a lot of musicians and songs that were happening through our church. So, my best friend and I were trying to strategize how to do it. Then one morning, we woke up at the same time and had this thought that he should be the CEO. That's Joel Taylor. So that morning, we started the record label. In the early days, we were super frugal and scrappy because we had to be. We did everything. We went on our first tour, and Joel did overheads, lighting, and helped critique the sound guy. And then I was out there during soundcheck telling the front-of-house guy what to do. We did everything from the artwork for the album to mixing the songs ourselves. We had a part-time intern who was 17 years old. Then right after that, we hired a part-time accountant. That was ten years ago, and now we have 120 staff members.

Finding your genius.

For all the worship leaders and musicians listening, it's important to understand that God wants to do a fresh and original thing with each person. Every person has a point of genius, and life is about finding what that is. At the same time, when you find your lane, don't knock someone else's. That's a big one because sometimes when we're young, we think we've found the secret, and we start acting like we know and we've got this new revelation. I see it all the time on social media. And I think to myself, *That's not a new revelation. That's been around forever.* So, having faithfulness and then figuring out what your sound, your lane, or what your God-given genius is, is really important. And I don't think you find that any other way than just keeping your head down and going forward. You will figure it out on the way.

Brian's struggles with depression and his family calling 911.

I've struggled with anxiety and depression since I was seven years old. A few years ago, that panic and anxiety that I thought I had beaten long ago began to haunt me again. So much so that my family had to call 911 because of a panic attack. I was feeling outside of myself and like I was spiraling into darkness. I talk about the whole story in my book, *When God Becomes Real*, and how worship brought me out of that. Anxiety, depression, and mental illness are an epidemic right now. It's a very common thing, and I want people who are having these struggles to know they aren't alone. When people feel like they're not alone, that's when they can reach out for real help. When you feel alone, you don't want to tell anyone about what you're going through because you don't feel like it's normal.

A lot of times, as leaders, we think we're protecting people by not sharing everything. We just want to be men and women of faith, so we don't share everything. And I get it; it's from a good heart. You want to protect people, and you want them to experience only faith. But at the same time, people are not idiots, and they're not as dumb as we may think. When you come out with what you're going through, there's a certain level of respect that occurs. You create a connection because everybody connects with a real story.

The Bible is all just stories. It's so funny when we get so intellectually smart, and we have all of our stuff figured out. We can do a five-point presentation or outline, but the Bible... all it is is stories and little teachings. I feel like we've got it backward. If we just tell our story and what we learned from it, people respond to that.

28

David Leonard

David Leonard is a Grammy-nominated quadruple threat. He's a songwriter, musician, artist, and producer. You may know him from his work as one-half of the duo All Sons & Daughters, where he's written "Great Are You Lord" along with many other songs impacting the church today. He has also toured as a keyboard player with Need To Breathe and co-owns The Creak Music and production studio in Nashville, TN.

IG: @davidleonardmusic

davidleonardmusic.com

Writing songs with a purpose.

All Sons & Daughters was birthed out of a small prayer group of twelve people. Leslie, the other half of All Sons & Daughters, just started writing songs about what we were going through and experiencing with our community. We never knew that people were going to be singing these songs outside of our four walls. Up until that point, I had written a lot of songs that were faceless. I was just writing songs to write songs. The revelation I had through All Sons & Daughters is God showing and telling me that "I know you want to create, you want to write, and you have the gifts to do those things, but let me show you that if you actually pinpoint who you create for, it has a greater impact than you just trying to throw something flippantly out there."

You have to put blinders on and figure out who you create music for and create music for them. If anything happens outside of it, awesome. But if it doesn't, you've created for the very purpose of hitting the need you set out to hit. Our need was our church. We were in a season of limits. We needed songs that allowed us to ask questions and declare what we wanted. So we wrote them. And what we didn't realize was that a lot of the global church needed the same things. And that's the beauty of God. Yes, dream big; I'm all for dreaming big, but at the same time, don't lose sight of the very things that made you do the things you do.

Why David can never write another "Great Are You Lord."

I learned that I would never be able to write another "Great Are You Lord" in my life. I know because I've tried. And after a song blows up like that, you come into writing sessions, and you're like, I have to have to write another one of those. But no one can do that. We had to get to the point of going, "Hey, our writing session is just for right now. Let's engage with this." Let's have an experience with God. If this is just for us in this space at this time, then let's do that. Let's engage with God in that way. Not feeling like we have to write some massive hit. Let's just have an experience with God right now. And that is so freeing, knowing that all I have to do is engage with God right now. I just have to have a conversation with Him. All this other stuff I can't control. I can't control who sings what or who does anything. There's no method to that madness. You can only respond to God and have a legitimate experience with Him. And that's the beauty.

We don't put as much weight on songs as I think we should.

It's so funny that we think songs are just songs. Sometimes God breathes some really, really special things, and a lot of it comes through songs. We're all moved emotionally or physically by what we hear, and music is a major part of that. We don't put as much weight on songs as I think we should. Yes, God is going to work whether or not we have songs, but I think He allows us to have these glimpses and moments of Him through song.

David's best advice for worship leaders and creatives.

I think if I had allowed myself to fail as a younger kid, I wouldn't have stressed myself out and worried as much as I did. Stress and the fear of failure kill creativity. If I had just allowed myself to take chances and be okay if it didn't work out. Then learn from it and move on. I would have given myself years back and been in a much healthier place.

So, as a creative or anybody who's trying to do this, allow yourself to fail at it because it's in the failing that we learn and grow. A lot of times in production, the best stuff comes out of accidents. Happy accidents. Something that isn't what you were trying to do, but it ends up being awesome. If you allow yourself the freedom in that, there's a real beauty that comes from it. So don't feel like you have to control it. Don't feel like you have to have every answer. Don't feel like you have to know every step that you're moving in. Just live in it, enjoy it, and soak up the happy accidents.

29

Mack Brock

Mack Brock is someone who's left such a mark on the worship community and is continuing to do so. He was a worship pastor, songwriter, and producer for Elevation Worship for over ten years and has written songs like "Here As In Heaven," Do It Again," "O Come To The Altar," "There Is A Cloud," "Give Me Faith," "Only King Forever," and many more. He is now releasing solo albums and has toured with some of the biggest names in Christian music.

IG: @mackbrock

mackbrock.com

Worship is the solution to doubt and anxiety.

One of the things I've learned is that walking in faith doesn't mean you don't have doubts or that you're not afraid, anxious, or any of the other stuff that comes with the territory. However, through worship, we can speak the things even if we're not even fully feeling in our hearts at the moment. For example, I can say in a worship experience, I've seen you win this battle already, and I've seen you victorious in this battle. And even if I currently have doubt in my heart, speaking that out loud can change our heart and our perception of our situations. We can also speak what we want our parts to be and pray where we want God to lead us. It's such a perception shift when we make proclamations through song.

For example, I think of one of the greatest hymns of all time, "I Surrender All." I bet if when we really examine our lives, a lot of us would really struggle with saying that and believing it, but it's where we all want to be. We want to be in a place where we can surrender it all to God. And so sometimes, just even singing "I Surrender All" creates a spark in our hearts that starts to chip away at things we've built up throughout our lives and lets God in. Worship and proclaiming God's goodness shift the posture of your heart.

Mack's best advice for worship leaders.

The biggest thing that worship leaders and musicians need to remember is that you're serving God's house and the people of God. The moment that you stop seeing the people you're serving as real people and individuals, that's when you start to head down a fruitless path. We're called to love people, and leading worship and serving them through music is just one way to love people. If it stops there, we're doing something wrong. To be more practical, I'd say really get involved wherever you're serving. Get to know the people you're serving. Get to know your community. Hear the stories of the people you're with to know how to serve them better. Then when you're leading worship or part of a worship experience, you're more aware of the atmosphere in the room. You're not just leading a crowd, but you're leading individual people who each have their own lives, problems, passions, and loves. Focus on that as much as you can, and you will have a much more fulfilling experience as a leader.

What to do when the congregation isn't worshiping.

Sometimes as worship leaders, we struggle because we want so bad to make sure that what we're doing is working. We have these weird checkpoints as to whether we're doing a good job or not. Things like whether they're raising their hands, they've got their eyes closed, or whether they're on their knees and crying. However, I've learned over the years to let go of my expectations of what it looks like for someone to receive. I had to let go of what I think a successful time of worship looks like.

It's a human tendency for us to try and mark whether we

did a good job or a bad job. It's a natural thing that I want to do, but I've just had to learn to let go of that and simply communicate as best I can. I'm going to speak the truth, and I'm going to try and shepherd the moment. What happens after that is out of my control. It's not something that I need to be consumed with.

We also have to remind ourselves that what we're seeing at face value is not always what's going on inside of someone's heart. There are so many times that I've been leading worship and noticed one person that I felt was not connected. And you can't help but keep looking at them and studying them. Then afterward we'll have a conversation with them and realize that the Lord is actually up to something inside of them. On the outside, it didn't seem like anything was happening, but on the inside, it was really special and powerful.

What Mack wishes he could tell his younger self about leading worship.

Early on, when I was in high school and just starting to lead worship, it felt very much like I was just singing songs. I was learning a song and singing the song, but it felt like something was lacking. One day I realized that maybe I should actually study what I'm saying. If I understand the songs that I'm leading, then I'll know how to communicate them to the people. Not only am I just going to let the song speak for itself in a sense, but I also want to be able to walk them through what we're singing. If I'm not connected to a song, how can I expect them to be?

For example, take the song "O Come To The Altar." This is what it means to say, "Jesus is calling you," to say, "leave behind your regrets and mistakes." It's one thing to communicate that in what you say, but I also think there's something to you carrying that in your spirit. There's a weight to that that translates the song at a different level. That's the biggest thing that I've worked on over the years. To really get a grasp on the heartbeat of the songs that we're singing, what they're actually saying, and trying to communicate that in the best way to the people we're leading.

30

Cody Carnes

Cody Carnes is a worship leader and songwriter who's written powerful church anthems like "Nothing Else," "Run To The Father," and "Christ Be Magnified," which are all a part of his Grammy-nominated record titled "Run To The Father". He's also co-written and recorded numerous songs with his wife, Kari Jobe, including the Grammy-nominated global anthem "The Blessing." He also serves at his home church, The Belonging Co. in Nashville, TN.

IG: @codycarnes

codycarnes.com

Growing up playing in Texas dance halls.

I grew up in a small west Texas town where everything was about football and oil. No one really cared much about music. I only started playing music because of my dad. He was a professional musician for 25 years and played country, southern gospel, and western swing.

I started playing drums with him when I was six years old. I would play a couple of songs when he would play weekend gigs with his friends at these Texas dance halls. My dad taught me how to play two songs: one was a shuffle beat, and the other was a waltz. He essentially taught me both grooves and where the stops were in the song.

There was a pretty funny gimmick that he would do in the middle of the show. He'd say, "All right, I'm going to bring my six-year-old son up now to play drums on 'San Antonio Rose.'" People were always amazed because I was so little. I couldn't even reach the bass pedal, so I would just lean against the seat to play those two songs. By the time I was ten, I was playing full four-hour gigs with him. And when I was thirteen, I started leading worship at my youth group. The rest is history.

Why worship music?

I love the idea of using music to connect with God. The thing that kept me doing worship was that I could create music and help people connect to God at the same time. To me, there's no better situation than that. This revelation sustained me through all the seasons of figuring out what I wanted to do, who I wanted to be, and who I was supposed to be. I love being creative, and God is a creative God. He wants us to have the freedom to be creative in our music. And the kingdom needs that creativity.

Creativity and the beauty of the local church.

When I was younger, my end goal was to get beyond the church and do something bigger. I'm not saying that you shouldn't chase those dreams, but be careful if they are only driven by the feeling that the grass is greener on the other side; it isn't. Creating music and doing it outside of the church is definitely needed, but it can feel lonely and depressing sometimes. It's a roller-coaster ride because your emotions are tied to it, and it's vulnerable. It's never fun to put your emotions out on a platter where someone on Instagram can so easily tear it down. As strong or as mature as I like to think that I am, there are days when that stuff really gets to me. I love the local church because it's the place you can always come back to. It's where you're known for who you are as a person and not just for what you've done. The local church is the best place if you're a musician and creative.

Writing new, fresh songs that are also familiar.

The sweet spot for creating music for the church is writing songs that the congregation will sing, but at the same time, pushing the creative boundaries so it feels fresh. My goal in creating music is to stay inside of the box but give the box some new colors and flavors. I think that's really where the impact is. Songwriting is a God-given desire because I think God understands that people need to hear something in a new way to awaken them and keep them from getting numb. And as far as the message of the songs we're writing, we're going to continue to write about the exact same story because the story never changes, and it's timeless. It will always be powerful, but it's still the same story. The interesting task that we have in front of us is that we're writing something new about the same story.

The beautiful thing about God is that His creativity is endless, and that's why people have been writing worship songs for over two thousand years. It's amazing that we still have new songs that make you say, "Wow, that's never been said before!" This will continue to happen for the rest of history. These types of songs awaken something in people's hearts. You know that feeling when you've heard a worship song that feels new to you in the way it grabs your heart versus when you've heard a song, and it doesn't really grab you.

I think for the sake of the church at large, not just for the sake of creative people getting their way, new songs have to be fresh. But at the same time, it has also to be familiar. It has to be something that they're going to sing at the top of their lungs that they believe and also has to be scripturally sound.

31

Sarah Reeves

Pop artist and songwriter Sarah Reeves signed her first record deal at age 18. For more than a decade, in addition to pursuing her own artistry, she has dedicated a vast portion of her career to writing songs for other artists, TV, and film. Her music has appeared in recent promos for "American Idol" and UFC and on television series across major networks like ABC, NBC, CBS, FOX, and Netflix, among others. She's amassed more than 41.3 million streams and over 33.4 million YouTube views to date. Although her personal style of music is pop, she also writes congregational worship music and leads worship at her local church, The Belonging Co. She's written songs for bands like Jesus Culture, Kari Jobe, Brandon Lake, and The Belonging Co.

IG: @sarahreevesmusic

sarahreevesmusic.com

Music background.

I grew up in a small town in Alabama and was raised in a family of musicians. I have three siblings, and we would always make music together. My dad was the worship leader at our church, and when I was twelve, I started playing piano in the services. He taught me how to play the piano and sing harmonies, and then it continued from there. I started leading worship in my youth group when I was 15, and we formed a little band that traveled locally.

My "big break."

When I was 17, we were opening at a festival for the headliner Plum. She didn't actually hear us perform that day, but we were around her and her crew. My dad came over to me and said, "Sarah, you should give her a copy of your CD." We had just made a little CD that my dad had produced and engineered. I said, "No, she's never gonna listen to it." However, my dad continued to encourage me, so I went over to the lead singer as she was getting in her van to go back to Nashville and said, "Wait! Plum, my dad wants me to give you a copy of my CD. You don't have to listen to it."

The very next day, she called and said, "Hey, I've never done this before, but I listened to your CD, and I was impressed. And I feel like I should help you." She and her husband brought me up to Nashville and took me under their wing. She introduced me to a ton of record labels, publishers, and management booking agents. This was all right after I graduated from high school. It was a whirlwind. I ended up signing with Sparrow when I was 18, did the touring life for three years, and then it all came crashing down.

It all came crashing down.

Because I was so young, I really didn't have much of a foundation and took the record deal and all the touring for granted. I ended up not being happy and leaving my label, thinking I would just go to another record label and get another deal. It didn't happen that way.

I went from touring to working at a daycare with kids. Through this experience, I learned a lot about humility, and God did a great work in my heart. In order to do work through me, He had to do work in me. As I look back, I know I wasn't ready for the platform. It would have destroyed me because I didn't have the foundation of who I was in Christ.

I thought my time as an artist was over, but maybe I could try songwriting. Songwriting has always been one of my passions before I was an artist or worship leader, and I thought that maybe I could become a songwriter for other artists. I started pursuing songwriting and worked on negotiating a publishing deal.

While working on an electronic pop song for another artist, I felt like God spoke to me and told me that I was not done as an artist. This gave me hope, so I started writing songs for myself again and dreaming about the future. He opened up so many new doors and surrounded me with like-minded musicians who helped me be where I am today. It was a huge story of redemption for me. I would eventually sign another deal seven years after I signed my first one.

Go to church. You won't regret it.

I could never do what I do by myself. I always say it takes an army of people to get where you want to go. Find a partner. Somebody that is different from you but has the same vision as you. For me, that's my husband, who is also my manager. I'm a dreamer, and he's a doer. He really helped me put together my creative team, production team, label, publishers, and all of my bookings. All of these different pieces came together to really support the vision I had. I couldn't do it by myself. None of us can.

It's so important that we are surrounded by a healthy community. I want to encourage every aspiring artist, leader, or whatever you do for a living to go to church. Don't miss out on it. It's important. As much as we think that we can do it on our own, there's something about getting together with the body and being in God's presence. It's so important that we are gleaning from the wisdom of leaders and being under a covering. It's something that I will always be a part of, no matter if I'm on the road or at home. It's so important that we go to church even when we aren't serving, singing, or playing an instrument on stage.

Tips on writing songs and staying creative.

Spend a lot of time writing and don't rush the process. Sometimes I'll spend a whole day working on a chorus, but at the end of the day, I'll do something amazing that I'm really proud of. Like any craft, the more you do something, the better you get at it. If you want to be a great songwriter, write a lot of songs.

Sometimes if I find myself in a rut, it's because I haven't been writing much. The more that I keep those creative juices flowing, the better. If you're a melody person, you can sing out melodies and record them on a voice memo on your phone. If you're a lyricist, you can open up your computer or your notepad and just write. Even if it's not a song, it could just be about your day, just keep creating.

Surround yourself with people that inspire you, even if it's just one person. Co-writing has been really good for me. I could write a song by myself, but having somebody else with a different perspective brings something I would have never thought of. You'll find new rhythms, melodies, chord progressions, or lyrics by having someone else work with you. Collaborating is a really great way to express songwriting, and it's so much fun.

Any style of music can be worship.

Listen to other people's music that inspires you. For a long time, I didn't really listen to music, and I wasn't really inspired to create music. When I hear other people making art and expressing themselves, it inspires me. Not to duplicate their sound, but to continue stretching myself to find new sounds. Listening to other genres of music outside of worship music really helps me become a better writer and musician.

I've always been inspired by pop music, but I felt like worship music had to sound a certain way and be relatable to every church for a long time. I felt creatively restricted because I felt like I had to write songs that fit into a certain mold and could be played during a service at any random church. I felt like God told me that I needed to be myself. He said that I would write songs that the church would sing, but I have to be true to myself and create my own sound with my own voice.

I love pop music, so why couldn't I do both? I started putting worship lyrics with pop sounds, and it is still worship. Who are we to say that worship has to sound a specific way? I want to encourage anybody that is a songwriter, aspiring artist, or worship leader to be themselves and bring what they have to offer to the table because that's what will inspire people. What you have to offer matters.

32

Phil Wickham

Phil Wickham is someone who radiates fascination with Jesus. He's a worship leader who has written songs that convey a yearning for intimacy and communion with the Lord. He's written songs like "Divine Romance," "You're Beautiful," "Desire," "Carry My Soul," and other incredible declarations that you're familiar with. He has also written anthems like "This Is Amazing Grace," "Battle Belongs," "Living Hope," and "House Of The Lord." His songs are being sung by millions of people around the world every single week.

IG: @philwickham

philwickham.com

Songwriting is work for me.

I've got friends that wake up from dreams, have songs in their hearts, then write them down and change the world. I would love for that to happen to me, but unfortunately, that's just not the case. It's work for me. Every song is different, but for the vast majority of songs, there's a real clear vision and moment of inspiration. Then chasing that down can take weeks, months, or sometimes a couple of years. I'll digest it, think it through, and figure it out until it finally lands. Then I can say, "Okay, this is what this was always supposed to be."

The job of the worship leader and how I write songs.

My parents are worship leaders as well, and ever since I was a little kid, they instilled this really big weight of responsibility in me. Just as the pastor teaches the word and is showing the heart of God, so is the worship leader. We're not necessarily leading in the teaching and study of the word, but you're pastoring the heart of the church into a deeper understanding of God's love for them. You're really pastoring the intimacy of the church as a group. Whoever's been given that 20, 30, 45, or even just 12 minutes of worship is a giant responsibility. This is when God wants people to be reminded of his greatness and respond to His goodness. It's a big deal to be a part of pastoring people into understanding and responding to that.

Then it's our job to write songs that cultivate that. Our songs have a goal to get people from point A to point B. Say I want to write the point A song which would be the first song in the set. I'll sit down and read through scriptures and get thoughts and ideas. I'll read about how Moses responded when God did amazing things. How did Mary respond when she was told that she was going to carry the son of God in her stomach? And you start to land on ideas and themes. So, now we're going to walk into this idea of how God has done amazing things for us so let's respond to Him.

Being present and remembering why we lead worship.

One week in church, we gave this altar call as a spur-of-the-moment thing. And literally, around 40 to 50 people came forward. Forty to fifty people said, "I want to follow Jesus for the first time." I remember looking down and casually thinking, *Sweet, this is cool. God, you're doing great things*, then just continued singing. However, I suddenly felt God saying, "Look down, look at these people."

So I did. And instead of seeing a group of forty people coming and going, I started looking at the individual faces that were so full of emotion, freedom, change, and joy. God was saying to my heart, "These are my children, and I have been waiting to be able to show them how much I love them their whole life. Now they're finally following me for the first time in their lives. They're finding a love that's not going to fail them, walk out on them, or get angry with them quickly. A love that's going to last forever, show them grace, and never give up on them."

I just was so overwhelmed by how God had shown me a glimpse of His massive love for these people. Forgive me for letting these moments become just a part of my culture and my vocabulary. We say things like "communion," "the cross," "eternity," "heaven," or "grace," and it so quickly can become just a part of our thing that we do. I want to fight so hard against that in my life by being in a constant state of wonder and excitement. I want to be in the moment and not miss out on what God is doing.

Best advice for aspiring worship leaders.

Ask God to give you a heart of humility and come into situations ready to serve. Leave your ego in the bed when you wake up. Don't even bring it with you. Don't even leave it at the door of the church. Leave it behind. Be humble and teachable. Put your own sensibilities, artistry, cool factor, and wanting to be just like Bethel or Hillsong aside, and ask, "How can I serve?"

Another thing is that many worship leaders have this mindset that they are going to leave the Bible study and knowing the word to the pastor. However, you need to know, understand, study, and have scripture hidden in your heart. Scripture needs to be coming out of you when you write. It has to be the foundation of your songs.

Be a person that stands in the authority that God has given you not to be timid, to lead, and not be afraid that you're too young or you're not good enough. Really step in with confidence, knowing it's not about what you bring to the situation that will change people's hearts. It's not about how good you are, how much you've practiced, or how great (or bad) your voices are. God is not reliant on those things to work. Facilitate the moment as best you can and watch God move.

The musical person's hack to a more intimate quiet time.

Music is a beautiful way to connect with God, but I find when I'm alone, I don't immediately go to my guitar, piano, singing, or to music. It's because I find myself getting too distracted with trying to write a new song or thinking of a set list. I need to walk away from that. My personal time of worship doesn't include music. Usually, it just includes intention. Instead of attending to the chords, melodies, my job, the setlist, or a new idea, I'm just going to give God attention right now. For some people, that might mean picking up a guitar, but for me, I find I'm less distracted when I leave the music out of my personal worship time.

33

Josh Baldwin

Josh Baldwin joined Bethel Music in 2014 as a worship leader and songwriter. Josh has written many powerful worship anthems like "Let the Redeemed," "Praises," "You Deserve It All," and "Stand in Your Love," which reached #2 on Christian Billboard charts. His songs carry a deep and unique perspective of Jesus.

IG: @joshbaldwin

Worship is prophetic.

Our pastor, he's always leading the songwriters and worship leaders in our church. And something he says is that we need to be writing songs that speak to where we want to see the church be in the next five or ten years. That's something I love to do. Yes, I want to write a song that helps people find words to say to the Lord and brings us together corporately, but also, how can I do it in a way that speaks to what we believe in, and moves us forward in our faith?

I think that's been happening more and more in church and in worship. I love that our songs can be about worshiping the Lord, but there can also be a prophetic nature to them that speaks to where we want to see ourselves in five to ten years.

Music can be used as this prophetic vehicle to speak to culture and speak to what the Lord wants to do. Because that message is through song and music, you can say tougher things and have it come across better or a little easier to swallow. You can get away with a lot more when something is packaged up in music. For instance, Bob Dylan, back in the day, he could get away with saying a lot of controversial things. But because it was wrapped up in music, it made the message easier to swallow. And there are tons of examples of that throughout history. That is something that I try to do. It's not something that's at the forefront of my mind when I'm writing because I know I'll overthink it, but it's something that I'm constantly aware of.

Writing worship songs that connect on a personal level.

I like to write songs that make worship a little more personal as you sing. For instance, the line "my fear doesn't stand a chance" from the song "Stand In Your Love." The one thing I kept wondering about was if I should say "my" fear. Do I want to own it? Or do I just say "fear" in general? There was this back and forth of questioning since we're singing it in corporate worship services. Do I want to own this? Am I taking too much ownership of something that I need to just give to the Lord? I finally came to the conclusion that there was something about making it personal. This is where people are, and this is where I am. Yes, Jesus died for everyone, but Jesus died for me.

I think about the woman in the back with her kids who's singing this song while going through whatever difficulties she may be facing. She can say, "my" fear, and the things that "I'm" struggling with, they don't have a chance. There is that tension that I come into battle with more and more in songwriting for the church where I want this song to be for churches all over the world to sing and connect with, but I also want it to speak to people personally. I don't want it to be this generic worship song. I want it to be something that an individual can grab onto and sing in their daily walk.

Songwriters—how to finish your songs.

Be more disciplined. Write often, even when you don't feel like it. Don't wait until you feel inspired. Develop and strengthen that muscle, and the inspiration will come as you're disciplining yourself. There's plenty of days when no inspiration comes, but I'm still doing the work. I'm still doing this because I know I'm called to do this. This is a passion, and more times than not, the inspiration does come. And when I get an idea or inspiration, now I know how to execute that idea because I've built the skill set. I can take those ideas, work them out, and craft them into songs.

Inspiration is the gun at the beginning of the race that gets us going, but discipline is what gets us to the finish line. And that's the difference between songs being just voice memos and songs actually getting finished. Inspiration sometimes ignites you, and other times, it finds you. More often than not, it finds you in the midst of your discipline.

34

Joth Hunt & Sam Evans

Joth Hunt and Samantha Evans are creative pastors, worship pastors, and songwriters at Planetshakers Church in Melbourne, Australia. They've been a part of creating over 30 internationally acclaimed albums, received numerous Dove Awards nominations, and have reached millions of people across the globe through their music and tours.

IG: @jothhunt

IG: @s_a_m_e_v_a_n_s

planetshakers.com

Joth – How to change the atmosphere of your church.

Praise, quite simply, is putting all the focus and attention on God. It's exalting Him and lifting Him up over everything we're going through. It's one of the best ways to start a church service and the best way to start your day. The Bible says, "Enter into His gates with thanksgiving, and into His courts with praise." So as we approach Him, the Bible teaches us to come with praise. It's the best thing that you can do no matter what season you're going through. Read through the Psalms. David constantly dedicates praise to God in the good times and the bad times. We personally have so many testimonies of praising Him in the hard times, and He brings a breakthrough. What I love about praise is that it changes the atmosphere of the room that you're in. God inhabits the praises of His people. So it sets up a great opportunity for Him to come and move. And regardless of all of that I just said, we do it because He's worthy of it.

Sam – Breaking off chains.

We've seen it. Praise has such a powerful, spiritual effect on people and atmospheres. And when people are going through a hard time, you put on the garment of praise, and it starts to have this effect upon your entire body, the way you feel, and the way you think. There are times when, of course, you don't feel like praising, and it's the last thing you want to do, but when you start to put on praise, it shifts you into a supernatural dimension. And this is where you can start to seek God with great freedom. It breaks off chains and heaviness. It puts you in a position where you're communicating directly to God. It's like a big vacuum cleaner that sucks out all the junk. Then you have this pure, clean pathway to God. Then you can have those very intimate, powerful moments with God.

Joth – Bringing the praise back to your church.

If you're a part of a worship team, hold that moment of praise in your service with such high regard because it does amazing things. I've seen and witnessed a lot of churches these days just opting out of doing praise songs for whatever reason. Maybe they're scared that the congregation will think it's too loud or too confronting in an energetic way, but don't lose that praise in your church service. Because, for starters, we want to do it because God is worthy of it. But secondly, it sets up an even greater worship time. When you get free in praise, you have an even deeper worship time. If you're a part of a church team, put some focus back on praise. Get some praise in your church, and let it be explosive. Let it be a celebration, let it be joyful, and let it be powerful.

Sam – "It's too loud, and you're just for young people."

Praise is a language of faith. Whenever we're singing our praise songs, we're using a language of declaration. We're praising Him like we've already got our miracle. And that's where we see these miracles break out in these spontaneous moments where the supernatural power of God is released into someone's life. As a band and as we've traveled, we have had negative reactions to Planetshakers. Things like "Oh, you're just for the young people," or "It's too loud." But, really, what we're also doing is giving God what He wants. He talks about clapping, shouting, musical instruments, and dancing. These are the things that are in the Bible. I want to give God what He delights in. And He delights in me using the language of faith in my circumstances and my entire body to give Him praise. And that's where we've seen so many powerful breakthroughs in people's lives. Because we're connecting with God in that way, he just starts moving spontaneously.

Joth –The importance of writing new songs at Planetshakers.

We do it because it's in the Bible, "Sing to the Lord a new song" (Psalms 33:3). Another reason is that we don't want to become stagnant. I think that is why it says in the Bible to sing a new song because God is always doing something new. Just like a preacher would get up and seek the Lord for a fresh word and preach a fresh message, that's how we view it with songs. We want to keep bringing a new song unto the Lord. We also don't just write songs about anything. We usually have themes in our songs. We like to partner with whatever Pastor Russell is preaching and write a song about that. This way, we can declare the word in the preaching and follow up with a song at the end of it.

It's also what it does in the atmosphere. A new song is quite amazing. If we haven't done a new song four weeks in a row, it starts to feel off in our church. A new song in our church and in our culture is so refreshing. Every song carries a different anointing or a different spirit about it. We're opening up new realms for God to move and bring revelation on new things. We also love to have fun in church.

35

Jon Foreman

Jon Foreman is the co-founder and lead vocalist for the Grammy-award-winning band Switchfoot. A band that, as most of you already know, has truly become a beacon of inspiration, love, and hope on a massive global scale. On top of releasing music with Switchfoot, he's been a successful solo artist for quite some time. To put it simply, Jon is a true legend. Not to mention, "Meant To Live" is the first song I ever learned how to play on the guitar.

IG: @jonforeman

jonforeman.com

Jon on the thing he's most proud of in his life.

We had an idea on a flight back to the States from Australia. We were tired from the tour and excited to be coming home finally. We were just really thankful to be alive, thankful to be coming home, and thankful for where we lived. We thought, how can we give back to the next generation? What would that look like? We thought to ourselves, well, surfing and rock & roll kind of kept us out of trouble when we were kids, so let's have a party with surfing and music on the beach and give money away to the homeless kids in our hometown. That idea became the BRO-AM.

The first year it started out with some friends from high school, just very grassroots and bare bones. And since then, it's grown to about 18,000 people on the beach every year. It's crazy, and every year I'm blown away by it. I'm way prouder of that than the Grammys we've won or any form of awards we've gotten. It's definitely one of our favorite things we've ever been a part of.

It's that classic wisdom—if you're passionate about something and you actually care deeply about what's happening, you're going to be invested in it naturally. And for me, music, surfing, and our hometown community are all three areas where I love investing my time, and I feel so rewarded by those pursuits. It felt like a very natural way to invest in the kids of the next generation.

Opening up for Bon Jovi, metal bands with real blood on stage, and playing Bar Mitzvahs.

We've opened for Napalm Death and even shared the stage with bands that used fake blood and real blood on stage. There are a lot of bands that would feel uncomfortable doing something like that, but the difference for us is that we play those shows intentionally. We play those uncomfortable shows on purpose. I think it's really interesting because over the years, we've opened for Bon Jovi in Europe in front of 70,000 people, played a ton of Christian festivals, and we've even played crappy little shows for two or three people. We've done it all.

Early on, you realize that as a band, your role is to bring light, to bring hope, to be salt, to be flavor, to be opening the doors and the windows of the souls of whoever might be listening to a bigger narrative than just yourself. And I feel like the irony is that occupation is needed everywhere.

Early on in Switchfoot's career, we'd play anywhere. We'd play frat parties, bar mitzvahs, youth groups, coffee shops… everywhere. It was this really beautiful commonality where you have this understanding that the youth group we're playing at is no different than the bar we just played last night. Everywhere, there are hurting people looking for hope and meaning. I'm reluctant ever to put a "we" and "them" in the narrative of whatever I'm saying. It's all "we," there is no "them." You are my brother, you are my sister. Let's talk this through together.

Being protested by Westboro Baptist.

Years ago, we were protested by Westboro Baptist, and I had this realization the day before that all the things that come against you in life are often the very chisels that God is using to reform you.

So, they showed up, and I had this completely different attitude. They were saying really derogatory, horrible things about us and about the people that were attending the show. I felt horrible for the people standing in line who were just being berated by this guy with a loudspeaker. However, I made the decision that I was going to give these guys water. So, I went across the street, and I gave him water. Then I said, "I just want to thank you for being here, and I'd like to take you guys out for coffee." Now every time since then when they protest, I get excited because I know this is something beautiful and an opportunity for God to use His chisel on me.

Responding to major disagreements.

I recently read a book that helped me understand why we struggle so much during disagreement or confrontation. It said that when someone comes in contact with a piece of information that challenges their ideals or their understanding of the world, many times their brain will actually no longer respond with the rational portion of their brain, and it just shifts into fight or flight.

So, when you're having a rational conversation with someone and suddenly it turns irrational, and you say, "What happened?", it helps me realize that I'm no longer talking to the rational portion of this human being. I'm talking to the fight-or-flight version. They've been challenged in such a way that they're actually fighting. That could be literal or figurative fighting. So, to answer the big question of how to respond in these situations, I think the only way through is love. I can admit that your love is the only thing that works on me when I'm challenged to such an extent that I'm willing to fight you over something. Love is the only thing that will win me over.

Say you have this rub with a person, and you think, "Oh, I hate this guy, he's the worst." But then he starts washing your car every Saturday. Well, eventually, you're going to actually take him seriously. His love will win you over. And I think that's what the cross is. They will know we are Christians by our love, not by our dogmatic theology. You might be right, but you're never going to win the argument without love. I believe it's in those moments of discourse that we're able to grow the most.

Responding to hurt people.

It's uncomfortable when somebody says to you, "I'm having trouble with this thing." Your knee-jerk reaction is to fix it, especially as a man and in my marriage. I'm quick to try and find a solution to the problem, but my wife tells me that

that's not helpful. She needs someone who can dive into the pain and say, "Hey, that must be really hard," and just sit there with her.

Job's friends sat with him for three days without saying anything. How many of us would have probably said something in the first 30 minutes? How often do we say something like "God is going to fix this" or "God is going to use this thing?" When the person really just wants to be heard and feel like they can be open and vulnerable with you.

It's okay to say, "I don't know."

In our post-Enlightenment, rational era, we feel the burden of having to know all the answers. But it's okay to say, "I don't know." We serve a God of mysteries. It's such a beautiful thing to say that my experience doesn't really have anything to bear on what you're talking about. I don't have the answers, but tell me more. I think it's a Christian response to admit that I'm bound by my own understanding of the world, and I'm still learning.

36

Jeremy Camp

Between 2002 and 2017, Jeremy Camp released 11 albums, four of them RIAA-certified as Gold. He has sold nearly five million albums and had 41 No. 1 radio hits. With those, he's garnered five Dove Awards, one Grammy nomination, three American Music Awards nominations, and four ASCAP Songwriter of the Year Awards. His 2017 album, "I Will Follow," debuted at #1 on the Billboard Top Christian Album and in the top 25 on Billboard Top 200. In 2010, Camp was named Billboard's #2 Christian artist of the decade. Jeremy is not just a legend in the industry, but he is a true artist that has given his life to using the arts and allowing his vulnerability to reach people in a deep way.

IG: @jeremycampofficial

jeremycamp.com

On losing his wife to cancer.

When you go through those tough times, you really gain an understanding of the Bible when it says, "He's near to the brokenhearted." Reading that and experiencing that are two different things. I remember when my wife Melissa went to heaven, I was in the hospital room, and I felt the presence of God so thick. I felt so close to Him like I never had in my life. I really experienced Him being close and near to the brokenhearted. I can honestly say that I was closest to the Lord in my hardest of trials.

A message to everyone going through pain and suffering.

Suffering is a necessary part of life. If there was no suffering, then we would not have forgiveness. It's because of Jesus's suffering on the cross that we have forgiveness. It's also okay when you're going through hard times to have those "why" questions. Jesus asked "why" on the cross, yet everyone's so afraid to ask the question "why." Jesus Himself cried out, "My God, my God, why have you forsaken me?" There's a freedom in realizing that if Jesus, who never did anything wrong, can ask "why," then it's okay for us to ask too. Be honest with God. Tell Him if you don't understand. Tell Him it hurts.

And once you've finally felt the freedom to ask "why," it's important that we don't stay there. What happens sometimes is we will stay in that "why" and never surrender to the "who." Even though I don't understand, I surrender to you, God. After Jesus asked why, He said, "Into your hands, I commit my spirit." So, I think that we miss the beauty and the refining power of suffering. Scripture tells us that as we go through suffering and trials, it's like gold being refined through fire. It's purified, and it's so necessary for growth in our life. We try to avoid it because we're afraid of pain, and pain is the thing that brought us life in the first place.

Jesus promised to walk through that pain with us. He didn't promise that we would not go through pain. He said, "I'll walk through that with you." I love the scripture in John 16, where it says, "I say these things to you that you'll have peace in this world. You will face trials of many kinds." He's telling us that when we go through tribulations, we shouldn't be surprised, "but take heart. I've overcome the world." That's the hope that we have. It's not that we're not going to go through trials and tribulations because He tells us we're going to. We live in a fallen world. However, he tells us it's okay and that we can take heart because He's overcome this world that causes those issues and causes that pain. He'll give you all that you need by sending His spirit to help you walk through those battles with His strength.

How to support those going through suffering.

As leaders, our teams and the people around us will go through tough times. The mark of a true leader is how you support your people. As someone who's gone through some tough times, I can tell you that the best thing you can do for your people is to simply be available for them. Sometimes, we're so caught up in the business of our life, ministry, and ourselves that we're not available. We try to make a quick fix. For instance, we'll talk to someone about what they're going through, which is great, but it doesn't stop there. When you walk with somebody, you actually walk with them through it. You don't just make a check in your check box and move on. People will say, "Hey, I love you" or "I will pray for you," check their box, and move on. If you're walking through something with somebody, it takes time, and it costs you something. That's a true measure of where your heart's desire is in walking alongside someone. Are you checking a box, or is it actually costing you something?

37

Amanda Lindsey Cook
—

In 2010, Amanda Lindsey Cook joined Bethel Music as a worship leader and songwriter. She's been prominently featured throughout the Bethel Music albums, as well as releasing three of her own solo albums. Some of the songs she's best known for are "You Make Me Brave," "Extravagant," "Starlight," "Pieces," and "I Will Exalt." In 2015, her first solo project, "Brave New World," won a GMA Dove Award for the most inspirational album of the year.

IG: @amandalindseycook

Writing songs that are "trying to be" worship songs.

I always wanted to write direct prayerful music because I grew up in the church, and I loved the idea of talking to God through music. But every time I tried writing, it always felt like, when I listened back, that I was listening to a song "trying to be" a worship song rather than just worship. I wanted it to just "be," but all I could hear was the "trying" rather than the "being." And because the framework of music for me was a place of absolute honesty, that was and has always been, the litmus test of whether or not a song feels good. And my songs didn't feel honest. So, it frustrated me to no end. I would sit down and try to write a song, listen back, and know that that's not even close to what my heart feels when I sing this song or when I connect to this song. Then there was a night when it started to click. I wasn't "trying to," I was just expressing. There was this moment when it became about the being and the expression rather than the "trying" to express it. Pretty quickly, the song "I Will Exalt" came out of that.

Worship leaders are soundtracks, not movies.

After we watch some of the best films, we walk away wanting to listen to the soundtrack. But not because we were listening to the soundtrack during the film. It was because something moved us, and the sound was so embedded into the story that we couldn't help but be impacted. It was a gentle impact. We never say, "Oh my gosh, that song took over the moment." The song only ever served the moment. So, we walk away wanting to listen to those soundtracks because they were so effective but subversive. The music in a worship gathering of people is to be a soundtrack that serves the purpose of the story being unfolded. We can all walk away with our own stories, and not, "That song was amazing." We want to have these epiphanies and experiences with God and then go back to the soundtrack because it supports and reminds us of what we experienced. The song wasn't the experience; it just had a supporting role. Our goal as worship leaders is to serve each other in that way. Worship leaders are to serve and create a soundtrack to someone else's expression, revelation, window into clarity, and communion with Christ. While not getting in the way or trying to become the main storyline.

Stop punishing your ego.

As worship leaders, we often struggle with our egos. How often are we condemned, or do we punish ourselves for having an ego? Probably a lot. But how often do we go to a place of healing our egoic selves, rather than punishing them? Rather than saying, "This song isn't worth anything because it had my ego involved." What if we looked at our ego with no shame? Then it becomes an opportunity to learn from and understand our egoic selves. We can ask, "Why do I feel like I need to hustle for something? What am I looking for?" By asking those questions, then we can write songs and lean into that space with healing.

Everyone is looking for a way to heal the wounded child that lives inside of us. We don't do that by creating an unattainable ideal. We do that by having a conversation with ourselves, with our wounded child, and with our previous ages trying to teach us something. We can then respond to that from a place of connection to the source. Then all the music counts, everything counts, all of it's unto something. All of it is meaningful now, rather than trying to get this utopian idea of humanity and trashing everything that doesn't reach that standard.

Sometimes we talk about how pure something is and imagine pure being the most clean or without sin. But the purity of a song is in how honest it is. And through waves of religion, it can sometimes be really hard to get to the bedrock of honesty that is our basis of spirituality and humanity. For songs to connect to people, they have to contain the humanity of the person who wrote them.

38

Sean Curran

Songwriter and worship leader Sean Curran was first known as a founding member of the Florida Christian rock band Bellarive. They hit the Billboard Christian albums chart with two albums in the 2010s before he joined Passion in 2017. He was featured on their song "Worthy of Your Name," which reached the Billboard Hot Christian Songs Top 30 in 2017. After appearing on Vertical Worship's "Real Thing" in 2018, he charted with Passion again in early 2019, with both "Welcome to the Healer" and "Bigger Than I Thought."

IG: @seancurran

seancurranmusic.com

Music teaches us how to talk to God.

When I think about the big "why" questions, especially when it comes to my relationship with music, it's simple. In the deepest way possible, I have no other answer for why music is a part of my life, except that God gave it to me to teach me how to talk to Him. It's how I find that space of intersection where broken things come together, where you can engage with mystery. Where mystery isn't something that scares you; it's something that beckons you. Music is that for me. I'm very grateful for it, and I think God does that for everybody. It doesn't have to be music, but for me, it's music.

Vulnerability is everything in leading worship and songwriting.

Vulnerability is the language of God. It's the only way we grow. Whether it's a great tragedy or great joy, it's the only thing in life that cracks us open and helps create space for coming together and connecting. It pulls us forward. We have these tendencies to recoil, shrink, or pull back to self-preservation. Doing that is what brings shame and fear. We get so good at building barricades around pieces of us that we don't want others to see, and we feel the need to look a certain way.

Vulnerability has a way of completely destroying the shame and fear that come with hiding parts of ourselves. It takes away all of the power that shame and fear have on our lives and helps us let those things go so we can grow. One of the things we can take from the resurrection is how saving the world required the creator of the world to become a helpless child. There's something about that vulnerability that lets us into the nature of God. It's the only way to see love and to see something real. It's become such a central piece of anything important.

I try very hard to have vulnerability be at the center of how I invite people to engage in a worship setting. The songs I write also help encourage that openness. It's not easy because I've found that the best way to activate that vulnerability is to lead with it. You can't ask people to do something you're not doing. You can't invite people to places you haven't been. It's the most disarming thing to say, "Here I am, take a look."

Growing up, I would spend a ton of time in my room with my guitar asking questions. What am I made of? What should I care about? What kind of thoughts should I have about my relationship with myself and with the people around me? Through that, I learned the language of God. I always felt safe, and He always pulled out of me the thing underneath the thing. He was always peeling layers away and calling me forward. His voice rejected the idea that I should keep padlocks on all my problems. This was a voice that said, "We're not going to do it that way. That's how you get stuck. So just hand it over to me, and we'll work through it together."

Being a worship leader who's not confident in singing.

It's funny that most of what I do now in front of people on stage is singing and leading worship. At least, that's what most people would associate me with. However, singing is the most uncomfortable thing that I do. It's the thing that I never asked to do, never wanted to do, and never felt confident doing. But such is the way of God to teach me a lot about His character and His nature by putting me in this space because that's what I do now. I sing. It's so fun watching God move through me. I've been forced to have an utter dependence on God when it comes to singing because it's not something I could do in my own strength. However, the guitar was. That's what I did. I played guitar for people. In college, I did session work. It's just what I did, and I was pretty competent. The moral of the story is not to let the gifting lead the story but to let the anointing lead the story.

The things we say on stage that place a divide between us and the people.

I would even encourage that you start to recognize how relatable it is to be vulnerable in any form of leadership, or even relationship for that matter. Then you'll start being able to bring that out in other people. I even try to be cautious of my language on a Sunday morning. By no means should you feel any shame if you've ever said this because I've said it too. But why do we say things like, "Hey, I don't know what you're going through this morning, but trust me, God's good." Why do we put that distance there? We don't have to do that. We can go about this in a different way. We can say, "Guys, I had a tough day yesterday, and some of it's still sticking with me. And I'm pretty sure that there are other people in here that can relate to that, but let's think about the hope that we're holding on to. Let's think about the hope that's bigger than this because we're singing about a story that's bigger than that." Then all of a sudden, there's no space between you and the people. You're acknowledging that we're coming in from different worlds, but there's not any divide or that somehow this person on the stage with the spotlight on them doesn't get you.

Because people are already thinking that. They think that the guy up on stage doesn't know anything about them and can't relate to them at all. And when we say, "I don't know what you're going through today," it just affirms it. I'm challenging myself as well. Let's go after that connectedness. If there's fear, shame, insecurity, or heartbreak inside of you, and you're not addressing it, it's controlling you and every decision you make in that place. You're giving that stuff a seat at the table when it shouldn't have one. There's an opportunity for us to lead the way with vulnerability so others can let go of what they're holding on to as well. Then God will show up in a big way.

39

Andrew Holt
—

Andrew Holt is the worship pastor at The Belonging Co. in Nashville, TN. Being at The Belonging Co. since the beginning, he has experience in what it takes to build a healthy church and worship team culture while modeling what it looks like to lead in authority and also submit to authority. He's also been a key part of writing and leading worship on The Belonging Co. albums.

IG: @andrew__holt

thebelonging.co

Building a family dynamic in your worship team.

Building a healthy team culture starts with how you establish your relationship with those joining your team. Early on, we make sure to connect with their story, spend time with them, and have multiple hangouts. We want each new member to understand that God has something way bigger for them than just being on our team. Our priority is that they get filled up here, find their people here, and get a renewed sense of passion for the presence of God. They can then take that into where they live. We establish that priority of relationship from day one. My goal is to look around on stage and confidently be able to say that I know everyone up here with me. I know their story, and I know what's going on in their lives. From that place, we can lead the rest of our family in the congregation into the presence of God. The goal of any worship team should be to care more about their hearts than what they bring to the table. Then prove that to them in the rhythm of the relationship you have with them.

Healthily approaching excellence.

Healthily approaching excellence is all about your priority list. The first priority for us as a church is for people to encounter and lift up the name of Jesus. Our second priority is excellence. We simply ask ourselves, "How do we keep Jesus, people, and encounter the number one priority, AND do it with excellence?" The moment excellence compromises our number one priority, then we know we need to make an adjustment.

We also know that we aren't going to get it 100% right every time, and we are okay with that. Inevitably, we're going to be tempted to stray from that. Which is why you constantly have to do check-ins and reevaluate by asking the questions, "Are we prioritizing presence over presentation, intimacy over industry, people over position, encounter over entertainment, and Jesus over everything?" And in the times when we get off, we figure out why then adjust and realign.

Another thing that plays an important role in having a healthy culture of excellence is that when something does go wrong, and it will, our first priority remains our first priority. A few years ago, we built this new Ableton rig and the guy running it made an error that threw off the tracks and caused a major distraction. When we got off stage, he was apologizing profusely. I looked at him and said, "Bro, was the name of Jesus lifted up, and did people encounter him? Yes? Then we won!" Once the emotions subsided, we later looked at the Ableton rig and made adjustments. However, in that moment when something happened that wasn't excellent to us, we were intentional not to allow priority number two to overshadow our accomplishment of priority number one.

Leadership that makes people scared to mess up, not take

risks, and become performance-driven and over-focused on encounters with Jesus stifles creativity and growth. It also abandons the one to reach the ninety-nine, and that is not God's heart.

40

Aaron Ivey

Aaron Ivey is a songwriter and worship pastor at Austin Stone Church in Austin, TX. Besides putting out albums through Austin Stone Worship that are reaching the nations, Aaron has a deep love for his home community and developing a healthy worship culture within his church and team.

IG: @aaroniveyatx

aaronivey.com

Leaders are distractible.

Eugene Peterson, on being a leader, said, "Jesus was always distractible by people." He was never so focused on his agenda or where he was going that he couldn't be distracted by any human being. You think about when he's going through the crowds, and somebody reaches out and grabs him, he wasn't un-distractible. He always took a moment actually to see, look eye to eye, touch, and be present with someone. As leaders, we should be distractible. We should have moments and time in our calendar when people can have access to us without it being a scheduled request or an email you have to send. That's what I hope to be—somebody that can not be so focused on what's coming up next that I miss the real moments where I get to actually be in people's lives and be like Jesus to people.

It's easy to be so focused on the work "of" ministry and neglect the ministry itself. Ministry is people. When you're trying to be productive, efficient, and get things done, you can easily do that at the cost of people. It takes discipline, self-awareness, and being intentional about "wasting time" with people. We start every single one of our weekly creative team meetings with 30 minutes of "wasting time." It's scheduled into the meeting. We may have food or coffee, but there's no agenda during that time. It's 30 minutes of people being human beings. You're not a minister, you're not a pastor, you're just a human being. That's been really helpful for people to know that this isn't an agenda or a religious thing. This is human beings together, serving the church, loving Jesus, and loving each other.

Developing a healthy team culture.

First and foremost, as a leader, you're always creating some sort of culture. So, if you're asking the question, "How do I create a culture?" or "How do I foster culture?", you're asking the wrong question because you already are. It could be a healthy culture or an unhealthy one, but whether you think you are or not, you're always fostering some sort of culture. Cultures exist everywhere around us—your college dorm, apartment complex, with your family, or with your friends. Every person that's in some sort of leadership position is, by their very nature, creating and fostering culture. So, your first question should be, "What kind of culture am I fostering?"

The word culture can be confusing or this ambient thing that makes us wonder what it even is. I think about some organizations that I would be tempted to say have a good culture. It's usually because they have good branding, their environment is awesome, or they have a slick website—for instance, Apple. When you go into the Apple store, it's tempting to think that this is great culture because it looks cool, smells great, or all of the people are wearing the same shirts. Those things are great; however, that's not culture. Culture is how human beings interact with each other.

This can be really freeing if you're at a church that doesn't have many resources. You don't have to have money, slick branding, or flash to have a healthy culture.

Culture starts with how people feel and how they interact with each other. So, the questions you can ask your team to determine your culture are, "What does it feel like to be on this team? Do you feel loved? Do you feel used? Do you feel valued? Do you feel taken advantage of? Do you feel empowered? Or do you feel bored?" How much of your time, as a leader, is spent not on the external stuff like making things look cool or sound cool, but on how your people are treating each other? Are you treating each other like Christ would treat His church? Are you choosing comradery over comparison? Are you choosing servanthood over stardom? Are we focused on the right things? Because having that right, is what good culture is. Regardless of who's there or how many resources you have, you can have an amazing culture when you focus on how people interact.

Developing a worship team manifesto.

At Austin Stone Worship, we have what we call a manifesto. It's just ten very short, simple statements. It's the guidelines of the type of people that we want to be as a team. Whether you're a volunteer or a staff member, this manifesto is how we want to interact with each other. The manifesto has nothing to do with what we produce or what we create. It's all about culture and what happens behind the scenes. I mentioned a couple of them earlier (under developing a healthy team culture), but some more are "We choose the Word of God over the words of people." What does that Word of God say about us, not the words of man?

Another one is "We depend on the power of the spirit rather than our own power." That's game-changing for a group of creatives. I'm going to depend on the Holy Spirit, not the spirit of Aaron Ivey, because that will always get me in trouble. Some more are "We love and worship Jesus above everything else," "We are a community of shepherds." "We choose servanthood over stardom," "We strive for excellence, not perfection," "We are not moved by applause or criticism." And I mentioned this one already, "We choose comradery over comparison." This is a huge one, "We focus on character over competence." We're going to focus on having good character, not being the best musician or singer that the world has ever seen. Then the last one is, "We consider others more important than ourselves."

We want to give to other people what we most desire for ourselves. Philippians 2:4 says, "Put aside yourself and help others get ahead." If there's a culture where a group of people are saying, "How can I get to a place where you are more important than me? How can I elevate you? I want to cheer you on. I consider you more important than myself," that's the start of an amazing culture of people serving the church together. If we had that kind of lens, not only would we have a beautiful culture, but that's the kind of power that changes the world. It's the Jesus way; that's what He did.

We use those ten statements everywhere. They're on t-shirts, our website, every email, spoken at every team event in some form or fashion. We just keep putting that in front of our people by

communicating that vision in a creative and compelling way over and over again. And over time, it just starts to stick.

A message to those discouraged about their team culture.

Shepherding people is not a quick fix. There's no instant gratification. It's this very slow journey of guiding people toward something. So, what I would say to somebody who feels stuck or discouraged right now is that you're totally normal. You're not a bad leader. You're not a doubting leader. You're just a leader. You may be frustrated and discouraged that your team isn't what you want them to be yet, but stick with it, be faithful. Faithfulness is so much more important than fruitfulness.

41

Danny Gokey

As a top-3 finalist on Season Eight of American Idol, Danny Gokey quickly became a favorite of millions. Following Idol, Gokey dropped his first album, "My Best Days," which debuted at #4 on the Billboard Top 200 albums chart. Danny has cemented his place on the radio charts with multi-week, multi-chart top-ten runs in the United States, Canada, and now Latin markets with his Spanish singles. He has been honored with three Grammy nominations, three wins as KLOVE Male Vocalist of the Year, two Dove Awards and numerous Dove Awards nominations. Church has always come before music to Danny, so he has remained very involved at his home church and worship team throughout this time.

IG: @dannygokey

dannygokey.com

Don't be a worship harasser, do this instead.

A lot of times, as worship leaders, we want to see results. If we don't see the results, we start doing what I like to call "worship harassment." We start telling people to try harder or press in harder. Our job isn't to be a worship harasser. Our job is to set an atmosphere of faith. What's the only thing that pleases God? Faith. So, as you're worshiping, and as you're setting the tone, how can you start making faith statements or faith declarations that will begin to bring the walls down of people? We do it with words. Words are capsules that contain images. So, when we're singing songs about God's love for us, it's replacing the image inside of us that God is angry with us. And when we're singing about how we're overcomers, we replace the image inside of us that were failures. Use your words and use the songs to build faith because that's what pleases God and allows miracles to happen.

The one who knows he's loved by God isn't even thinking about the enemy.

David says, "Come magnify the Lord with me." The word "magnify" is interesting to me because if you were to put a magnifying glass over anything, it would become really big. But it's not actually getting bigger; it just appears bigger and allows us to see it more clearly. Whatever you're holding the magnifying glass to, that thing is going to become clearer and in focus. So, when you magnify God, we know He's not actually getting bigger; He's already big. But in that process, you're taking the magnifying glass off of your problems and putting it on God. He starts to become bigger in your life, and our problems become smaller. You start realizing that God is bigger than your problems. God is great and greatly to be praised.

If you only knew how many times I would try to go into worship from a sincere place, with the intention to tell God how much I love Him. Yet, sometimes we have to make space and allow God to tell us how much he loves us. If you remember, Peter was the one who declared his love for God yet was the first one to fail. Peter was an emotional guy. As worshipers, we can relate to that. We're all so ready to convince God of our love, rally the troops, and fight. However, if we take a look at John, he wasn't the one trying to prove himself to Jesus, yet he was the disciple whom Jesus loved. It's because John had the magnifying glass on God's love for him. John was the one that was reclining on Jesus' chest.

Jesus asked Peter, "Do you love me?" three times. And Peter said yes each time. Then Jesus began to prophesy about Peter. Immediately, Peter pointed at John and said, "Well, what about him?" Jesus basically told him, "Don't worry about him; you follow me." Jesus had to keep redirecting the passionate Peter just to follow Him and not worry about everyone else. However, you notice that Jesus never had to do that with John. Remember, John was always the disciple that Jesus loved. There's something about coming to a place and just receiving, knowing that you're loved unconditionally. That will put you in a place of worship where you're not always trying to be up on the stage fighting and trying to crush the enemy. The one who knows that he, or she, is loved by God is not even thinking of the enemy. Even though Hell might be breaking loose, he rests in knowing that God's love is greater than life.

When you start realizing what Christ has already done, you'll stop fighting and trying to obtain victory or your position as a son or daughter. You start realizing, I am already victorious. Then you realize you're seated in heavenly places, so you start worshiping like you're there, whether you feel it or not. You know what He said, and you can worship from that place. It's more of a thanksgiving type of worship. Which is how we enter his gates, with thanksgiving and his courts with praise. That is the kind of worship that God wants.

42

Judah Akers

Judah Akers is most known as the frontman for the band "Judah & the Lion." Early on, Judah consistently refused opportunities to create secular music because he only ever wanted to be a worship leader. God spoke to him one day and told him that he was "putting God in a box," thus the band was born. Although being a secular band, the heart of Judah & the Lion is to spread the love of God to the masses and to those who would never step foot into a church. And they've been doing just that, having toured with bands like Twenty One Pilots, Incubus, Jimmy Eat World, and KALEO. Their recent album "Take It All Back" topped the alternative charts for three weeks straight.

IG: @judahandthelion

judahandthelion.com

Showing the love of God in a secular world.

I experienced God's love at a young age. I went through some things in my early twenties that forced me to grow up really quickly. My parents just went through a really hard divorce in a very explosive way that ripped our entire family apart. We had overdoses, suicides; you name it. All that to say, it's in those moments where you can discover true love and true hope. I thought that I had true hope already, but honestly, I didn't know the half of it until I went through those tough times. So, my story is one of God pulling me through the darkest times, and that gives you profound empathy for other people.

So, when we play shows, we hear a lot of stories of what people are going through. To me, it doesn't matter what they believe; I don't care where they're coming from or who they are. The thing that connects us is the brokenness that makes us human beings. There's nothing like the love of God. The scripture says they won't know you by your works. They won't know you by your amazing preaching or your amazing singing. They will know you by your love. And that's what I want the message of my life to be. I want to represent God's love wherever I go. You don't have to be screaming the name of Jesus to show what the heart of God looks like.

It's always been about people and the love and unity that we can share as humans, which obviously, for me, is rooted in faith. When you pair that with empathy, you just love people because they're human and deserve love. We do that with no agenda or even being in a position where we're trying to change that person. We have so many people that come up, and they're really struggling either mentally or physically. Our goal is to try and put it in their bones how much they're loved and cared for as humans. It's the most important thing to me.

A message to church leaders.

When I was in college, I had the mindset that I needed to save everyone around me or that I always needed to be doing more. However, there was a real God-given moment that I can point to that gave me a revelation. During this time in college, our friend group was experiencing amazing things. A lot of people were being healed, giving their lives to God, and there was testimony after testimony. We had a buddy of ours in our friend group who came in and got saved and baptized. We asked him about what it was that made him want to give his life to Christ. We thought, of course, it had to be the healings or the amazing testimonies, right? Well, I'll never forget his answer. He said, "No, you guys just really love each other well."

That moment really affected my heart. God is so much bigger than what we know. Yes, the way that we lead and what we speak on stage is important. But none of that means anything if you don't have love and acceptance in your community. The Bible says that gentleness leads us to repentance, not fear, and not boldness. I would encourage church leaders, and everyone really, to allow the love of God to completely infiltrate you. Then operate and respond to people out of that manner. That has always been the better response for me. It's not on us to change someone. Anytime you come in with an ulterior motive or agenda, that's not true love. That's like saying, "I know how to fix you." When you come to people, especially outside of the church, without an agenda and you just try to love them well, that is much more powerful than anything else we could do. "I'm right, and you're wrong" never works.

43

Mia Fieldes

Mia Fieldes is a Grammy-nominated worship leader and songwriter from Australia. She spent ten years as part of Hillsong Church before moving to Nashville and becoming part of The Belonging Co. in 2017. Mia has collaborated with some of today's top Christian artists, including Michael W. Smith, Francesca Battistelli, The Newsboys, Meredith Andrews, For King & Country, Zach Williams, Paul Baloche, Matt Maher, Chris Tomlin, Kari Jobe, Passion, Jesus Culture, Bethel, House Fires, Lauren Daigle, and The Belonging Cø. Some of the songs written by Mia include "Christ is Risen," "Peace Be Still," "Fierce," "Tremble," "Yes I Will," and no. 1 radio hits "He Knows My Name," "Chainbreaker," and "First."

IG: @miafieldes

Mia gets right to the point.

The first thing I'll say if you're interested in writing songs is that I'm a big believer that anybody can write a song. But I also think the people who have the most fruit as far as songs go are the people who work at it. For example, you can't get mad at the guy who always gets the opportunity to play guitar when he practices his guitar five hours a day. I think there is something in the church where anyone can participate. However, if you want an opportunity, God is a promoter, and He honors hard work. I think one of the best stories in the Bible is about the person who buries their gifts. What happens to him? Sorry, but he gets cut out. And the person that's a great steward, God gives you more.

How relationships influence your songwriting.

The importance of relationships in my songwriting can't be understated. It's important to make sure that you love the people before you love a song or a moment. It's about putting value on what God puts value on. And that is family, people, and relationships. He died for a relationship with us. It wasn't for songs; it was for a relationship. So, if you love people and you put value on that first, it's amazing how God will connect the dots.

I have a lot of writer friends, and I love getting to be a part of their seasons. You get to stand beside them and pray with them through things that are really hard. There've been seasons that my writer friends have helped me sing through. And there have been seasons that I've helped them sing through with a particular song they needed in that season. It's way easier to come into a writer's room and know that Franny, for example, is in this season, so we can write songs that prophesy over that season. Or I know that Chris Quilala has just gone through this tough thing. So, let's write songs that speak into that and prophesy something different. There's so much power in singing over yourself. Worship really is warfare. And you don't war alone. Nobody does. It's always an army taking on something bigger than themselves. Sometimes you send people to the frontline in one area, and sometimes you send them to the frontline in another area. It's amazing to be able to be a part of everybody's journey and to sing something that is for that person but also for the greater army.

One process isn't better than another.

When I started writing the song "Fierce," it wasn't like we were on the floor crying and having a moment. I was literally watching an episode of America's Next Top Model. Tara kept saying everything was fierce, and I thought, *Yeah. I don't even think you know what that word means.* I don't even know what it means. So, I looked up the word fierce, and one of the translations was "to pursue with intensity." Straight away, I thought about the story of the protocol's son. And I often will connect the idea to someone I know. So, for this, I thought about my friend Chris who has this real authority when he sings about the love of God. That is one of the lanes that he runs in and is just really good at. He has this authority because every time he sings about it, you feel it. So, I wrote his name down, wrote the word fierce next to it, saved it, then later connected with a friend, and we wrote the song in forty minutes.

That's to say, I don't think that experience is any less holy than a song that was written with me lying on the floor crying. God anoints hearts, and He uses different songs in different ways. It's easy to believe that God anoints some songs and doesn't anoint others, but I don't think that's true. God anoints hearts, and He uses things in different ways. It takes the pressure off of us trying to write the next most anointed song. No, just write songs that prophesied over your season. Write songs that tell people what's true. Write songs that help people and serve what they do.

Putting faith in people's mouths.

When David in the Bible wrote a lament, it always finished with, "but God." He would end with how God overcame. We see a lot of songs where people talk about how they feel or what they're facing, but there's no "but God." I don't think it's bad to process feelings, but you have a responsibility if this is a song you're putting in people's mouths. You have to make sure what you're giving people is faith. That's not to say it has to be "happy-clappy" or that you disregard feelings, but we need to leave people with faith.

At the end of the day, I don't want to be saying everything sucks, or I'm a dirty rotten sinner because that's just not true. The Bible says I'm the righteousness of Christ. You can feel something, but just make sure you're always finishing with "but God." Especially if it's for a corporate setting.

44

Kristian Stanfill

Kristian Stanfill is a worship leader, songwriter, and worship pastor at Passion City Church. He's most known for his involvement with the Passion Band, as well as releasing his own solo worship albums. He's written worship anthems like "Glorious Day," "Lord I Need You," and "Always."

IG: @KPStanfill

Six years of writing terrible songs, until...

I started playing guitar and writing songs when I was around 13. The songs I was writing were terrible. They were the worst things you've ever heard. It was around that time that I started really falling in love with God as well. I didn't know what a worship leader even was then or what they did. There was no template I was trying to follow. My youth pastor heard I was playing guitar a little bit and told me, "You're a worship leader now." So, I was thrown into the fire and had to figure it out. This can be one of the best ways for it to happen because you don't really have time to overthink it. And through that, we started seeing some pretty phenomenal stuff happen in our youth group. I was hooked at that point. I knew that God was doing something special, and I loved being a part of leading people into his presence and calling out worship from people.

Fast-forward to college, and I was still writing terrible songs. During this time, I met my wife, and something clicked for me. I was falling in love, and it was the most real thing I'd experienced in my life up to that point besides God. So, I started writing songs for her. In the process of falling in love, I was writing her these songs that were raw and real. Writing a worship song and being in love with Jesus, without trying to trivialize it, it's the same thing. I want to write this real expressive love to God. That was where something clicked into place for me, where I started understanding how to express my love for God and his grace with honesty.

Stop floating around, and get planted.

Being a part of Passion for as many years as my wife and I have has been an incredible ride. There's something really powerful about sticking in one place for a long time and being in it with people through the ups and downs of seasons. There's pain and heartache, but you also get to experience the highest mountains and breakthroughs with people.

If you're jumping around from place to place, church to church, movement to movement, looking for the perfect organization, you're not going to find it. Every church and organization is made up of people, and people are broken and imperfect. You're going to have hang-ups wherever you go. However, it's only when you plant and let your roots go deep that you can weather any storm. Our relationships with the people around us are tried, tested, deep, and authentic. I don't want to try and do that anywhere else.

I'm not saying that God doesn't call people away from places. Sure He does. And I'm not going to say that's not in our family's future. But if we do go, it will be under the leadership and under the authority of my pastor. I can't say how valuable it has been to have that.

For a long time, I was a worship leader without roots. I would go wherever the wind blew. I would go do this over here, and I'd go to this church over here. If I was in church on Sunday, great. If I was leading somewhere out of state, that'd be great too. I found that to be a really unhealthy rhythm for my family and me. I had no real community, accountability, or pastoral leadership in my life. And that is just a recipe for disaster. We need an anchor and to be grounded and rooted. That's what our church has been, and I can't imagine what we would have missed if we had just floated around.

Stop using your team members.

Leading people is the best part of what we do, but it's also the hardest part. You get to experience the highest joy with people, but at the same time, you're showing up in the really hard stuff when people are crying and broken. And it's more than just showing up and being available; it's making sure that people know they're not being used. People know when they're being used and when you just want them to execute a song, fill a position, or fill a role. People need to know that they're part of this team and part of the story that God's telling in this church. We need to make sure that people feel that and understand they play a unique role in what we're doing. That can sound like just words, but the way that it becomes more is when people feel like they're being pastored, shepherded, and we know their lives.

Our worship team is really big at Passion City Church. We've grown a lot, and there's no way for me, as the worship pastor, to be able to have a touch on everybody. But our worship staff is amazing, and we have leaders on our team that can reach out and make sure everybody has a touchpoint. Making sure people feel valued, cared for, known, and seen, is the most important thing to me as a leader. We spend a lot of time talking about this because it is the hardest thing to do on a team.

Conclusion

Thank you so much for reading. This book may be finished, but I challenge you to continue pursuing your journey of growth. If there's a mentor from this book that you really enjoyed reading about, go check out any other content they may have available. If you want more content on worship leadership, vocals, or instrumentation, we have a ton of high-quality resources at WorshipOnline.com.

CONTINUE YOUR
JOURNEY OF GROWTH

NEVER SHOW UP UNPREPARED ON SUNDAY AGAIN

Perfectly learn your parts for Sunday in half the time! Guaranteed. Get instant access to video tutorials/lessons that cover the exact song parts so you and your band sound incredible while eliminating stress, and increasing your confidence on stage!

See how easy it is to get back hours of your time and sound incredible doing it!

 Enhance your culture of excellence

 Eliminate the guesswork

 Play/Sing with confidence

Start your free trial at
WorshipOnline.com